THE SECRETS
TO
NONVIOLENT
PROSPERITY

The Principles of Liberty

TREVOR Z. GAMBLE

Published 2011 Trevor Z. Gamble

Cover art by Vincent Saldaña

ISBN: 1466477857
ISBN-13: 978-1466477858

DEDICATION

This book is dedicated to my dad, Foster Gamble, for always helping to stoke my natural curiosity, and for being an example of someone who isn't afraid to ask the big questions.

CONTENTS

ACKNOWLEDGMENTS

First and foremost, I'd like to thank my dad, for being my biggest supporter and encourager from day one of writing this book. There were a number of times where I was either stuck or had given up, and he managed to convey to me the value he saw in what I was doing, which inspired me to finish it. I'd like to thank Kimberly Gamble, for reading and commenting on several drafts, helping to bring to the writing a more compassionate voice than I had been incorporating. I'd like to thank my mom, Dania Moss, for giving me her comments on a draft. I know it wasn't easy to get through, but hopefully your feedback has made it more accessible to others. I so appreciate the works of Murray Rothbard, Ludwig von Mises, Stefan Molyneux and Hans Hoppe, among many, many others. This writing is standing on the shoulders of hundreds of years of thinkers, and I am grateful for their contributions.

Chapter 1

DISCOVERING THE SECRETS

It is my passion for life and compassion for human suffering which compel me to write this book. It is my desire for people to be able to lead free lives, follow their passions, create thriving relationships, and pursue happiness which motivate me to get the following insights out.

When I was confronted with information about social and environmental issues I was not aware of - the population bomb, climate change, pollution, increasing poverty and illness, etc. - I realized I needed to get involved and make a difference. Why were so many people suffering? Why was the environment being degraded so rapidly? I became active in trying to find solutions to these problems.

I discovered that much of what I had been taught about the state of the world and the causes of various problems was simply wrong. Many of my beliefs were being shaken up by the new information I was finding. I was on a quest to learn what was really going on. What are the causes of the problems people experience, and what can we do to alleviate them?

I came to find out that not everything is as it seems; that the problems are not just accidental, but are actually linked together like streams in a delta flowing from a river, where fundamental issues lead to many downstream problems. The source of this river, as I came to find out, was the beliefs which would allow certain political and economic policies to exist.

My interest lies in swimming upstream so that I can strike at the root of the problems. These chapters contain the most important insights I have come across which I want to share with you, in hopes of a better world.

I know that many people's eyes glaze over when they hear the words "philosophy" or "economics". You may have the view that philosophy is a collection of abstract musings by dead white guys and that economics is better left to the Harvard Ph.D's. Well, it is my intention for this book to turn those perspectives upside-down. All of the ideas that I will be presenting you will easily be able to relate to your own life; you will see their importance, and you won't have to do any math (okay, there is a tiny bit just for illustrative purposes).

There is tremendous power in having certain knowledge and there's a reason the secrets in this book are not widely known and discussed. These secrets fundamentally empower you, while many of the popular economic doctrines and political ideologies are ones which disempower the individual and empower a small, elite group.

The following insights, which lay out the moral and economic cases for complete liberty, are not new with me, as many great thinkers have already contributed thorough works on these topics. I wrote this book because I saw a need for a more user-friendly introduction to the philosophy of complete liberty and free market economics. While I tried to anticipate and answer many of the primary questions I believed people would ask when reading this book, this is not intended to be an exhaustive treatise, but rather an accessible primer.

* * *

It's true - nonviolent prosperity is possible, and I even believe that it is likely in the future. This is not just being free of the mafia, common burglars or identity thieves, it is a much greater freedom as well as a much greater prosperity. It is the freedom to live your life as you choose so long as you do not harm others. The fundamental question, which acts as the premise for this book is, "How do I improve my situation without violating *anyone*?" Many people might respond that they are not violating anyone, but we live in a world where the violations of people's property rights are so commonplace that we do not even recognize what we are doing to others. I will be pointing out these acts of force so that we can become aware of them, and make the conscious choice to relate to one another peacefully through voluntary exchange.

This is a book about my search for truth, which can be challenging to uncover amidst the propaganda in much of the media. Fortunately, the internet makes this search easier for all of us. You may be exposed to some ideas in this book which you have not thought about before, or which conflict with your current beliefs. I encourage you to keep an open mind, and follow the logic and evidence. The quest to learn what is really going on in this world has challenged my beliefs repeatedly, and when I have seen the fallacies of what I was holding on to, I have let them go.

For many it may be hard to believe, as it was for me, that there have always been, and probably always will be, some people who want to have power over others. Fortunately, they are a tiny minority. Those who have been successful in gaining this control, whether they are royal families, dictators or even representatives in a large democracy, tend to be the minority of the population. For the vast majority this is not the case, and therefore it can be difficult to relate to that ideology.

There is a story about how to boil a frog that you have probably heard. If you put a frog into boiling water it will jump out right away, but if you put it in cool water and warm it up slowly, the frog will not detect the temperature increase and will gradually burn to death. As gruesome as that story is there is a direct parallel to human beings. Those with the power to control other people's lives, liberty and property are always in the minority. Because of this, they realize that to stay in power they cannot use direct force, but rather must use psychology to change the beliefs of the people so that they will ask, and even demand, to be controlled.

> I am freeing man from the restraints of an intelligence that has taken charge, from the dirty and degrading self-mortifications of a chimera called conscience and morality, and from the demands of a freedom and personal independence which only a few can bear.
>
> Adolf Hitler,
> German Nazi leader, 1934

> ...a long habit of not thinking a thing wrong, gives it a superficial appearance of being right, and raises at first a formidable outcry in defense of custom.
>
> Thomas Paine,
> American revolutionary, 1776

Hitler, Stalin and Zedong did not kill those millions of people personally, they convinced others to do it. Those others were "just taking orders". If all of those nameless killers were not convinced, and did not think that was the right course of action, then these supposedly powerful people would be reduced to insignificance. But because of people's complicity, terror reigned down on millions.

While this is an extreme example, the same willingness to take other people's property without clearly thinking about it or by "just taking orders" is pervasive in our society.

> Wishing to be free, I cannot be, because all the men around me do not yet wish to be free, and, not wishing it, they become instruments of my oppression. The true, human liberty of a single individual implies the emancipation of all; because...I cannot be, feel, and know myself really, completely free, if I am not surrounded by men as free as myself, and because the slavery of each is my slavery.
>
> Mikhail Bakunin,
Russian revolutionary, 1867

The only way that those in power have maintained their positions is because other people are not willing to think for themselves and to take responsibility for their actions.

> If the communists have succeeded in strengthening their power in Russia, Cuba and Ethiopia, it's because they found sufficient numbers of volunteers in those countries to accomplish the task of hangmen while the rest of the population did not resist. And all of them are responsible - all except those who died while resisting.
>
> Alexander Solzhenitsyn,
Russian novelist, 1982

There is a pervasive sense of anxiety these days regarding the state of the economy and people's relationship with government. While many cannot pinpoint the exact problem, they know something is terribly wrong. There is a general feeling of helplessness and disempowerment as most people are forced to suffer the consequences of the actions of a small number of people.

While some Americans are starting to become disillusioned, most still believe that we live in a free country under the free enterprise system with a big government that is well-meaning and good, there to protect us and take care of our needs.

> The people will never give up their liberties but under some delusion.
>
> Edmund Burke,
> Irish philosopher, 1784

It is no coincidence that the most limited government in history became the largest. The United States, at its founding, was a much more business friendly place than other countries around the world. This allowed businesses to flourish, and the growing revenues for the private sector meant growing taxes for the government. And thus what started out as the freest country has slowly grown to control many aspects of peoples lives both in the United States and in other countries, with its 735 military bases around the world. Many people think that to have freedom we just need to limit government, but that has been tried, and we are now living with the consequences. Governments give us freedom on a leash. They don't want it too tight or people will rebel. They don't want it too loose or people will realize they don't need a government. They want people to be just free enough so that they are productive, thereby feeding the government.

This book is not about taking sides, left or right. These deceptive distinctions are pitting people against one another and keeping us from uniting and looking at the core issues. Rather than the traditional left/right spectrum, where you would have the communist, Stalin, on the left and the fascist, Hitler, on the right, we will use a different spectrum, with the range from ultimate power over yourself on one end to someone else having ultimate power over you on the other end. This is the meaningful distinction, because now you get the collectivist ideologies of mass murderers such as Stalin and Hitler together on one side, and the individualist philosophy of most honest people who just want to go about their lives without being hassled on the other side.

I will show how property rights have been misunderstood and disregarded, and that it is time for us to lift off our blinders and start respecting one another's property. The longer we lay asleep, ignorant of these rights, the more challenging it will be to reclaim our liberty. Because actions tend to follow beliefs, this book will look at the core beliefs which effect us all, explaining the different sides so that you can entertain the logical conclusion that nobody but you should be in control of you.

The general rise in people's standard of living has led many to think this will continue on automatically. This is a fallacy. We must understand just what makes an economy grow as well as what inhibits growth and causes an economy to contract. This book explores those issues which are the keys to sustaining our prosperity and unleashing a whole new level of wealth in the world. We must first unleash ourselves so we can be free to pursue our self-interests in voluntary cooperation with others.

I recognize how painful it can be to confront information which shakes up the core of everything we have known and valued, and in many cases devoted our lives to. I imagine that a young reader may have an easier time with the information simply because there has been less time invested in what may inadvertently have been a self-destructive path. But whether young or old, we are confronted with a choice to value truth or stability. The way out of the challenging times we are facing now may call into question the value of our life's work and beliefs.

I welcome your participation in the following intellectual and emotional journey. I know from personal experience that it can be a very challenging one, but at the same time it is an exciting feeling to be onto something that is true. I stumbled upon the secrets scattered here and there in different resources, where one insight would lead to my researching about another, until at last I got a more comprehensive picture. It is that picture that I am sharing with you here. These secrets are the keys to nonviolent prosperity for us all. It is my intent to reveal these great insights so that we may all benefit.

I started out by saying that my love of life compels me to write this book. I am convinced that the understanding and application of the principles in this book are the best ways for people to live the lives they truly desire.

Chapter 2

RIGHTS ALL A JUMBLE

Where I used to live in Jackson County, Oregon, there was a pretty hot issue that many people were up in arms about. They were taking to the streets in marches, sending out pamphlets and making unsolicited calls trying to get people to vote for more taxes to reopen the public libraries. All fifteen libraries in the county had closed due to a long-foreseen end to federal funding. Those in favor of the new library levy claimed that information should be free and that it was their right and their children's right to have a "free" library. Those who opposed the levy were not opposed to libraries themselves, but rather to how those ones were funded. If a lot of people want libraries, they will spring up and meet people's needs in the free market without the need for coercion. There was also a privately owned library of which I was a member, which was not having any funding issues. In fact, they were constantly expanding the number of items they carried and services they provided, while charging a minimal fee.

With the two sides battling over this issue, it was clear that there was confusion about what rights are and where they come from. These days "rights" means many different things to different people. Some people say they have a right to clean air and water, to food and shelter, to education and a good income, to job security, welfare and healthcare, while others say they have the right to their private property, and for others not to aggress against them or their property.

There are clear distinctions between these perspectives on rights that I will elaborate on shortly, but why are we starting out exploring rights? I have found that by becoming clear about this topic, many of the difficult circumstances people are in and the issues which many people most care about, such as poverty, world hunger and our impact on the environment, become easier to understand and improve.

A DARK POSSIBILITY

Okay, now close your eyes… just kidding. But I do want you to imagine a scenario here: you are living in a society where you are not allowed to own anything, not even your body. There are laws which dictate what you can do and how you can live, prohibiting you from engaging in many voluntary actions. This is a repressive and authoritarian society in which every aspect of your life is controlled by others. This oppressive world is reminiscent of the rigid lives that people were forced to lead in George Orwell's novel *1984*.

> Never again will you be capable of ordinary human feeling. Everything will be dead inside you. Never again will you be capable of love, or friendship, or joy of living, or laughter, or curiosity, or courage, or integrity. You will be hollow. We shall squeeze you empty and then we shall fill you with ourselves... If you want a picture of the future, imagine a boot stamping on a human face — forever.
>
> George Orwell, *1984,* 1949

We were the first to assert that the more complicated
the forms assumed by civilization, the more
restricted the freedom of the individual must
become.

Benito Mussolini,
Italian Fascist leader, 1929

As we will be exploring in this chapter, there is a critical
dichotomy between a world where we own ourselves and one in
which others claim to own and control us. It is important to
recognize this distinction and allow our minds to envision what life
would be like in each of these scenarios. Why should we concern
ourselves with what life could be like in the future? In the short
term, many people are willing to give up their rights for a belief of
enhanced security. But if we take a longer perspective, we can see
how our rights are increasingly being treated as negotiable. The
dark possibility certainly is not inevitable, but we are headed in a
direction of more and more control over our lives being in hands
other than our own. Keep that vision in mind as we continue the
discussion of what our rights are.

TRUTH

What is objectively true is true, regardless of whether or not
anyone believes it. A majority of people leading their lives
believing that 2+2=5 does not make it so. But the consequences are
very different depending on whether or not what you believe in is
the truth. If you are trying to fly to the moon, but your calculations
are incorrect, rather than gently landing, the spacecraft is likely to
crash into or completely miss the moon. The same is the case for
rights, and that is why it is of utmost importance for people to
become clear about what rights are and what they are not. As our
true rights are getting eroded and forgotten, there are dire

consequences which can lead in a downward spiral to the imagined dark possibility.

> Truth is whatever benefits the State; error is whatever does not benefit the State.
>
> Robert Ley,
> Nazi Minister, 1890-1945

> To make a contented slave, it is necessary to make a thoughtless one and to annihilate the power of reason. He must be able to detect no inconsistencies in slavery, he must be made to feel that slavery is right.
>
> Frederick Douglass,
> Abolition leader, 1818-1895

So What Are Rights, Anyway?

First of all, I will ask the question, "Who owns you?" The answer may seem obvious, that you own yourself, but with this answer, there are tremendous implications. What are the alternatives to owning yourself? Two other options are that everyone owns an equal part in everyone else, or there are select individuals which own the others.

The situation where an elite group, king or master has ruling authority over the rest of the people has arisen many times in history. The general population are second-class people without rights of their own, left to the mercy of the ruling class. This was the situation with slavery in early America. The slaves were not seen as having rights of their own, and that is how people were able to justify buying and selling them as property. Where does this view come from? For ages there have been some people who believed that there were those more naturally gifted and that they should be the rulers. The rulers then have the incentive to look for differences between themselves and the masses so that they can keep the power. But this means that there are no universal human rights. Your rights may not be the same from day to day and from place to place.

Now let's take the case where everyone owns an equal part in everyone else. For anyone to take any action, they would first have to get approval from everyone else. This may seem possible in very small groups like a family, but we must think a little deeper. Even the action of asking the others for permission is an individual act, as would be someone else's decision to give permission or not. To take it one step further, how could one person own a share in every other person without first owning one's self? What is it that would be owning those shares?

> Every man holds his property subject to the general right of the community to regulate its use to whatever degree the public welfare may require it.
>
> Theodore Roosevelt,
> U.S. President, 1910

Imagine today having to get agreement from the other 6.9 billion people on the planet before you ate a sandwich, bought a car or had a child. Obviously this could not work, and that is why in places where this is attempted, the population is divided into two groups, with one telling the other what they are allowed to do, what they can eat, what they can buy, etc. While many see communism as an ideal, you can see how it is logically impossible for any action to occur because no individual can take initiative. And thus the ideal of communism leads to the same situation as the first example, where an elite group controls the rights of the rest of the people.

CASE STUDY: *How Socialism Leads to Class Societies*

Let's first consider how a country can become socialist, meaning that nobody owns property. The peaceful way toward complete socialism is to patiently wait for everyone to voluntarily donate their property to the state, whose stated purpose it is to divide the resources for the common good. These people would have to wait forever because not everyone would want to voluntarily give up their property and put their trust in the state. The other way is to forcibly take away people's property, either by passing laws which prohibit private ownership of property or by using direct violence to force compliance.

> I believe that in every part of our complicated social fabric there must be either national or state control.
>
> Theodore Roosevelt,
> U.S. President, 1910

> Your America is doing many things in the economic field which we found out caused us so much trouble. You are trying to control people's lives. And no country can do that part way. I tried and it failed. Nor can any country do it all the way either. I tried that, too, and it failed. You are no better planners than we... Will it be as it has always been that countries will not learn from the mistake of others and will continue to make the mistakes of others all over again?
>
> Herman Goering,
> Nazi Minister, 1946

Violent taking of people's property is what has occurred in every instance that socialism has been instituted. While it can be easy to start a small socialist society with 30 or so people who voluntarily donate their property, when the numbers become large - like thousands, millions or hundreds of millions - forceful taking of property becomes necessary for socialism to succeed because there are always people who on some level understand the nature of property ownership. Nazi Germany, Soviet Russia, Communist China, Communist Cuba, and all of the other Communist-bloc countries have resorted to violence in pursuit of their ideals.

> The so-called socialist ownership is a disguise for the real ownership by the political bureaucracy.
> Milovan Djilas,
> Former Yugoslav communist, 1957

Since people are divorced from their property, an individual or group of people have to make decisions about what resources should go where. Thus the people of the country are divided into decision-making and non-decision-making groups, with the first group having power over the second, and getting special treatment. In Soviet Russia, one's rank in the government or Communist Party would determine the grade of housing one got and whether or not one could get an automobile.

Forced labor is common, and necessary in fully socialist countries, because it follows that as the state needs to plan the economy, it also needs to plan the jobs in that economy. There were 20 to 30 million slave laborers in the infamous Gulag system during the Stalin years in Soviet Russia. And those living on collective farms - as many as 40% - were prohibited from moving away without permission from the collective farm management. It becomes apparent that in a state of socialism, the average person becomes a means to an end for the rulers.

> Every Communist must grasp the truth! Political
> power grows out of the barrel of a gun.
>
> Mao Zedong,
> Chinese Communist revolutionary, 1938

There seem to be just two options then. Either you own yourself, or someone else does. Put this way, people might want to take back control of their lives when the options are so clear. For example, would you like to spend the money you earn as you see fit, or would you rather someone else had that authority? Would you rather have control over where your child gets educated or would you prefer someone else decide? Some people may not want the burden of so much responsibility, but many others would appreciate the newfound freedom. Even if you don't want that responsibility, you cannot justly force others to give up theirs.

> Socialism of any type leads to a total destruction of
> the human spirit and to a leveling of mankind unto
> death.
>
> Alexander Solzhenitsyn,
> Russian novelist, 1978

So we arrive at the 1st Rule of economist Hans Hoppe's Four Rules for private property: *We own our own bodies.*

The alternative to this is slavery. The only way you can argue this point is by having control of your body, and thereby ownership. Let's say you propose this concept to me, and I flat out refuse to accept it, boldly sharing how we all own one another. What would you say to that? You would simply point out that by stating my position I was exercising control over my body. I did not have to consult with everyone else on my answer or lack of it. The action I took was independent, and thus I have control and ownership of my own body.

SELF-OWNERSHIP

Self-ownership is both the option that actually works and a true statement about reality, but what does it entail? Okay, so we've determined that you own your body and mind, and thus you have one fundamental human right: you have the right to live your life as you choose, so long as you do not infringe on the equal rights of others. There are an infinite number of implications: you can eat what you want, do to your land as you please, buy and sell what you like, etc. In this system every action is voluntary. I may not initiate force or the threat of force against another person or their property.

> If we are self-owners, neither an individual, nor a majority, nor a government can have rights of ownership in other men.
>
> Auberon Herbert,
> English philosopher, 1897

> From a socialist point of view, it is quite senseless for a separate member of society to look on his body as his own private property, for an individual is only an isolated point in the transition of the race from the present to the future.
>
> Preobrazhensky, 1927

What are some further implications of self-ownership? Well, you have freedom of conscience, freedom of speech, and personal freedom. The freedoms are unlimited so long as they are on your private property, or you have the agreement to use someone else's property for your desired actions. People have the right to think whatever they want, have different religious beliefs or scientific theories, and they have the right to express that to others. They can talk, write, or broadcast over radio, television or the internet. As long as they have justly acquired the rights to use the different media, then they may say what they want.

> The only enlightening way of analyzing economic
> and property problems is by always returning to the
> individual who, alone, is real.
>
> James Sadowsky,
> American philosopher, 1966

PRIVATE PROPERTY

But wait a minute, isn't the right to live different than the right to own property? First, let me define property as anything that people can use, control and dispose of. While humans are amazing creatures, we are not self-sufficient. We need to cultivate land to grow food and use resources to make shelter and clothes and so on. While we may choose to use minimal resources, our livelihood is always dependent upon things we need which are outside of our bodies. The freedom of thought and action allows people to secure the means for their survival.

An example here might help to illustrate this point. Say I parachute into a jungle uninhabited by humans and I need to find food and water before I perish. I pick fruit off some trees and gather water in big leaves. I then make a place to sleep for the night out of grasses and tree branches. I have put my work into the land and have thus altered it. What I changed is now mine. If another person walks up to me, they cannot justly claim ownership over what I have created, but I can give what I have for free, trade for something he has, or simply keep my creations for myself, all of which is voluntary. In order to secure my well being I need to interact with the world. And thus property rights are a direct extension of being a rational self-owner.

> Abolition of all property in land and application of all rents of land to public purposes.
>
> 1st plank of communism:
> *The Communist Manifesto*,
> Karl Marx & Friedrich Engels, 1848

> No human rights can exist without property rights. Since material goods are produced by the mind and effort of individual men, and are needed to sustain their lives, if the producer does not own the result of his effort, he does not own his life. To deny property rights means to turn men into property owned by the state. Whoever claims the 'right' to 'redistribute' the wealth produced by others is claiming the 'right' to treat human beings as [slaves].
>
> Ayn Rand,
> Philosopher and novelist, 1962

We live in a world of limited goods, meaning we cannot satisfy all of our wants, and we thus have to make choices based on what is most important to us. As we progress, and our basic needs are met, our desires also tend to expand. While it is very easy to imagine things we might like to have - a luxury car, a private jet, a yacht - it takes time and labor to create these. Thus, most people's desires will perpetually be beyond what they can actually satisfy. If we were not faced with scarcity, then property rights would not be an issue because there would be enough to satisfy everyone's wants for everything, immediately.

While some propose that technological advances will allow us to live in a utopia where everyone's desires are satisfied and there is no scarcity, they are ignoring that these advancements will also lead to increased desires for things which would still be scarce, such as each person having their own rocket ship or second home on Mars. Now back to planet Earth, where goods are scarce compared to people's desires, and thus property rights are of utmost importance. As long as scarcity exits, property rights can never be abolished, despite the wishes of many. An individual or group of individuals always has control over a good.

This brings us to the 2nd Rule: *We have the right to own previously unowned property. The first person to mix his or her labor with property is the rightful owner.*

What would the alternative be? Maybe the second, third or one-hundredth person to come to the property is the rightful owner. The consequences would be dire if this rule were not true because people would lose their incentive to make unused land and resources productive.

Imagine what would occur if the law of the land stated that the 100th person to touch a piece of property was the owner. Say I found a piece of land that I liked that had never been used. I alter it appropriately to make it ready for the home I am going to build. Once it's done, people start coming onto the land and into the house, changing things here and there, hoping to be the 100th person. I would not be able to live on the land or sell it because I would not be the owner. For how long would I continue this charity of clearing land and building homes only to have others appropriate them from me? Most people would probably spend their time going around touching things hoping to add to their small collection. You can see that there is no logical reason that any arbitrary number, other than the first to mix his labor with the resources, should be the rightful owner.

The 3rd Rule states: *What I produce with my labor and my property is also my property.*

Who else should own what you produce with your own labor and your own materials? If someone could just come along and take what you have spent time and energy creating, then obviously this would dramatically decrease one's incentive to produce in the first place.

And the 4th Rule: *As the owner, I can transfer goods as I see fit.*
Who else should get to transfer the goods? If people did not have the right to exchange goods that they produced at their discretion, then this also would lead to far less being produced.

These four rules are the foundation of liberty and security, and thereby, prosperity.

> Liberty is not a means to a higher political end. It is itself the highest political end.
>
> Lord Acton,
> English writer, 1907

"HUMAN RIGHTS" ARE PROPERTY RIGHTS

As odd as it may sound at first, human rights are property rights. When something is your property, you may dispose with it as you please. This is not a right *of* the property, or *belonging to* the property, but rather the right *to* the property, to use it as you see fit as long as you have acquired it justly.

All human rights can be boiled down to property rights. In a society based on property rights (not our current one) I can do what I like in my own home, but what about when I am on someone else's property? Let's take a look at a supposed limit on free speech. According to Justice Oliver Wendell Holmes, people do not have the right to falsely shout "Fire!" in a crowded theater. If we look at this example from the standpoint of property rights, free speech has not been violated. If the person yelled "Fire!" and there was no fire, then he would be acting against the rules of the theater, and would have to justly compensate the owner for the lost business. If the owner yelled "Fire!" then the customers would be the ones who should be compensated because it was in their implicit contract that they would be able to enjoy the showing for the fee they paid. People's right to free speech is not as unlimited as many would like to believe. If your webpage goes against the specified standards of the hosting company, they can take it down because it is on their property. When the property is your own, you can do with it what you like. And when it is someone else's you can do what is allowed by your contract.

EQUALITY OF RIGHTS VS. EQUALITY OF MEANS

If someone acquires property justly, then that person may give it to someone else or exchange it for another person's legitimately acquired property. This concept of private property and voluntary exchange disrupts any patterns of coercive wealth distribution. Suppose we have a society where the wealth is distributed exactly as you would like it to be: in this case, an equal amount for everyone. You come out with a fantastic new invention, and people flock to the stores to buy your $10 widget. After the first weekend, you sell 100,000 of them. In a very simplistic way, let's say you now have $1million more, and all of those people who bought your product now each have $10 less. The wealth equality has been disrupted, but what's the problem? You got your money legitimately because each person bought your product voluntarily, showing that any pattern will be disrupted through voluntary exchange, and that this is a wonderful thing. You only became wealthier because you satisfied the needs of many people.

An exchange only takes place if each person involved believes they will be better off after the trade than before. Each person perceives that they are getting something of greater value than what they are giving up.

> The value of an article does not depend on its essential nature but on the estimation of men, even if that estimation be foolish.
>
> Diego de Covorrabias,
> Spanish lawyer, 1512-1572

In our example then, you are able to make your $1 million because you gave more than $1 million in value to your customers. In this way you can see how your invention did not take a piece out of the pie, but rather increased the overall level of wealth and value in the economy. You effectively made each dollar worth more than before. The size of the "pie" increases as more people's needs and desires are met through voluntary exchange.

The pattern that does emerge will be constantly changing as people choose what to do with their property. But isn't there a serious social problem if they are super-rich? The question is not how rich, but rather how was the money acquired? If the money was acquired through force or the threat of force, then that person is not the rightful owner of that money. But if you get wealthy by selling something to people that they voluntarily exchange their money for, then you are only growing wealthy by satisfying people's preferences and giving them what they want. Remember, in order for someone to have $1 billion in a truly free market, he had to add more than that amount of value to people's lives.

This brings us to the point of inheritance. Is it fair for anybody, but particularly those of great wealth, to leave all of their money to their children, giving those kids an obvious monetary advantage in life? This choice is no different than a wealthy person wanting to purchase a boat or a jet or donating to a charity, in that he is choosing to do with his money that which he most prefers. Once again, if he acquired it justly, then he can dispose of it as he sees fit. He can give it all to his children, or give some to his children, some to a charity, and some to a business. Rather than focusing on the recipient of the money or goods, we need to look at the giver. If someone received their money in an ethical way, then that person has the right to do with it as he pleases.

Money which is inherited, particularly large fortunes, is not simply consumed. Most of the money is in the form of investments in businesses, and it is these investments which allow for businesses to grow, resulting in increased consumption of better quality and lower priced products in the future.

> Abolition of all rights of inheritance.
> 3rd plank of communism,
> *The Communist Manifesto*,
> Karl Marx & Friedrich Engels, 1848

> The institution of inheritance powerfully promotes the accumulation of capital. It provides a motive to people to maintain their capital, and even to go on accumulating additional capital, as long as they live – for the sake of their heirs... Everyone in a division-of-labor society benefits from the existence

of this additional capital, whether he himself is an heir or not.

George Reisman, *Capitalism,* 1997

It is often asked or even demanded of people, once they have made their fortune, to give back. From the customer's perspective, the wealthy person has built his fortune by giving more value in products and/or services than he has received in money. Of course the businessman has the opposite perspective, that he has acquired more value than he has given. And that is how it is with all peaceful transactions.

Giving back and enriching people's lives is all the successful, ethical businessperson has done. He has the right to do with his money as he chooses, including giving to charities. But to demand that action of the successful is unfair and shortsighted.

RIGHTS VS. STATE-MANDATED ENTITLEMENTS

There are major problems today with what people are claiming as rights because many are not aware of the distinction between rights and state-mandated entitlements, which people often think are their rights. It is clear that we live in a world of limited goods, and in this world there are two ways for someone to improve their condition. The first is through work and voluntary exchange or gifts from someone engaged in the voluntary process, and the second is through theft or gifts from someone who steals. The second is often easier, particularly if you are taking from someone you do not know, but it is unjust. Though there may be short-run gains for the few, a society based on theft is certainly not on the road to prosperity. The incentive to innovate and produce is diminished if everyone is trying to live off the fruits of everyone else's labor in the form of demanding benefits from the government which are paid for through taxes.

> If some men are entitled by right to products of the work of others, it means that those others are deprived of rights and condemned to slave labor. Any alleged "right" of one man, which necessitates the violation of the rights of another, is not and cannot be a right. No man can have a right to impose an unchosen obligation, an unrewarded duty, or an involuntary servitude on another man. There can be no such thing as "the right to enslave".
>
> Ayn Rand,
> Philosopher and novelist, 1966

The first difference between a true right and a state-mandated entitlement is that a right is timeless. My right to my body and my life are the same rights now as they were 5,000 years ago and will be the same 5,000 years from now. Whether or not those rights have been and will be respected is a different story. The point is that these rights are not time dependent. Contrast that with the very time dependent entitlements to public transportation or a house. 5,000 years ago public transportation did not exist, and the houses certainly weren't much to talk about. In 5,000 years, public transportation hopefully will not exist, except as archaeological curiosities and no one knows what we will be living in. The point is that they cannot be a human right if the rights keep changing over time. It is then not a right of being human, but a state-mandated entitlement in a certain place and time period. To put it more bluntly, someone promoting entitlements might say, "I would like to live in a house, use public transportation and have my children educated at the local school, and have other people pay for it."

Preferences are great so long as they are attained in ethical ways; the problem arises when the force of government is used to manifest those preferences, turning them into state-mandated entitlements. Because every entitlement has an obligation attached to it, someone else must give something up in order for that person's "rights" to be met. This brings the distinction that rights are realistic while state-mandated entitlements are utopian. Everyone on the planet could have their rights respected in an instant with just an act of will; while for each person to have all of their entitlements would take an extraordinarily long time, if it would even be possible.

Now, say I think living in a house is my right, and that the government will back up that right by making other people accommodate it. The way that I will get that house is by other people paying for the construction of it. Thus, while I have become wealthier by having a house, all of the contributors to the house have become poorer. Every time a state-mandated entitlement is enforced, some people gain while others lose. Taking the public library example, the population has a state-mandated entitlement to the library. Those who choose to use it get the benefits, while everyone who pays property taxes is forced to pay the costs, even if they have no interest in the library.

Compare this situation with rights. If I have my property, others do not lose theirs. If I am voicing my opinion on my property, others are not barred from doing the same on theirs. If I engage in voluntary exchange - mutually agreed upon exchange of private property - others are not prohibited from engaging in the same activity. To clarify, if I was willing to give you $5 for a sandwich, and you were willing to sell your sandwich for $5, then we would mutually agree to the trade, and it would be voluntary. If, on the other hand, someone wanted the $5 sandwich, and forced me to pay for it, then that would not be a voluntary exchange, but rather a forced one in which property was unjustly taken from me.

In our day these economic truths have become accepted as self evident... Among these are: the right

*what do you think abt trade-based societies,
ie. Burning man?
* Animal rights - real or not?*

to a useful and remunerative job in the industries or
shops or farms or mines of the nation; the right to
earn enough to provide adequate food and clothing
and recreation; the right of every farmer to raise and
sell his products at a return which will give his
family a decent living...; the right of every family to
a decent home; the right to adequate medical care
and the opportunity to achieve and enjoy good
health...

Franklin D. Roosevelt,
U.S. President, 1944

Many of you may read the previous quote and feel this is a noble
perspective. While I agree with the objective of everyone's needs
being met, there are peaceful alternatives to using the violence of
government. As you read on in this book, it will be valuable to
consider this nonviolent approach when your reaction may be for
the government to solve our problems. These pertinent issues will
be explored throughout the book.

In this world of human rights, only humans can interfere with those
rights. If a vandal floods my house, I have the right to seek justice
since my property rights have been violated. Specifically, the
vandal would be liable for the damages. State-mandated
entitlements, on the other hand, do not limit themselves to human
involvement. If a hurricane flooded my house, many believe it
would be my "right" to have others pay for the rebuilding of my
house, even though no human was responsible. This means that
people are punished for actions for which they were not
responsible. This does not mean that because no one was
responsible that no one would help. Absolutely people would
contribute to getting those who are suffering back on their feet, as
they do now even while being heavily taxed.

ARE PROPERTY RIGHTS ETHICAL?

When studying ethics or economics, it is important to know that you are on solid ground in your logic. Hans Hoppe has elucidated the fundamental axiom of ethics, which states that *humans are capable of argumentation - or, proposing ideas - and thus knowing the meaning of truth and validity through this process.* Again, this is true because to try and deny it would be to argue and thus prove the axiom. Even choosing to ignore an argument or choosing to stand still and not "act" are still actions because they are conscious choices. Each conscious choice asserts one's control over one's mind and body. So ethics springs from the recognition of private property, first in the ownership of one's mind and body, and then to the property which the person justly acquires.

NON-AGGRESSION PRINCIPLE

From this clear logic about why property rights are just comes what is known as the non-aggression principle, that every person has the right to live his life as he sees fit, so long as he does not interfere with the equal rights of others. The corollary to this is that no one has the right to initiate aggression against another person or their property. This does not forbid self-defense, but it does forbid actions such as murder, rape, assault, robbery, kidnapping and fraud. You may wonder why fraud is included. Fraud is a form of theft because you are paying for one thing and receiving another, contrary to your contract. If you paid me for a Rolex, and I gave you a knock-off instead, I would have stolen the money you paid.

> Is freedom anything but the right to live as we wish?
> Nothing else!
>
> Epictetus,
> Greek philosopher, 50-120 A.D.

This is the fundamental principle for peaceful social dynamics, and if this is fully understood, then you don't need to read anymore. The rest of this book unpacks the implications and clears up misconceptions.

COLLECTIVISM

Collectivism is an ideology which values "society" or the "nation" above property rights and self ownership. It is this doctrine which denies all natural human rights and instead confers privileges to a select group. People are meant to sacrifice their own interests for the good of the group.

There are dangerous consequences of the collectivist doctrine. Since the group, such as a government, does not exist in reality, certain people have to be representatives for this fiction, thus gaining power over the real individuals. The majority elects people who are responsible for "guiding" the group, deciding what people can and cannot do. Inevitably, this ideology results in a few people controlling the many. Not only is this unethical, but when people are not able to fully enjoy the fruits of their labor, they are less inclined to be as creative and work as hard, thus preventing people from becoming as prosperous as they would in a free market.

MAJORITY RULES?

Individuals are the smallest units that have wills and make choices. In fact only individuals have these qualities. Thus the non-aggression principle applies to all individuals and organizations, which are composed of individuals. There are not greater rights that come to groups than to individuals because rights cannot be aggregated, meaning individual rights cannot be added onto one another to form bigger group rights. The rights of ten people do not outweigh the rights of one person. If they did, then human rights would not exist because they could always change by the will of the majority. Majorities cannot justly gang-up and take property from minorities, although that has happened throughout history and continues strongly in current times.

> We no longer believe that it is just for one man to govern two men, but we have yet to outgrow the absurd belief that it is just for two men to govern one man.
>
> Charles T. Sprading,
> Activist and writer, 1913

Let's take an extreme example so that you can see the fundamental problems with majority rule. Imagine a group of nine people select a child they want to use as a sacrifice. They don't want to be seen as barbarians, so they decide to include the mother in a vote. The mother has a tough choice ahead of her. She can put in her vote, knowing that she will probably lose 9-1. Or she can abstain from voting because the system is unjust, in which case the vote is 9-0. Either way, in a society where the majority rules, the child and the mother lose. In a private property based society, consenting adults could do with one another what they choose, but voting to take the life or property from another would be unethical, and not condoned.

> Remember also that the smallest minority on earth is the individual. Those who deny individual rights cannot claim to be defenders of minorities.
>
> Ayn Rand,
> Philosopher and novelist, 1962

While the above example may lead you to think of this situation as isolated cases of "mob rules", where the pitchfork and torch

*How to keep order if majority doesn't rule?

bearing members of the mob harass an individual or small group, this is in fact the basis of democracy. What you are allowed to do with your life and your property are strictly regulated by the will of the majority. Many people believe that a democracy is the greatest political system because each person gets a voice with their vote, either directly on a measure or by voting for a representative. While it can be better to have a voice than none at all, these systems are founded upon the denial of self-ownership. In a democracy, no person has inherent rights - it is up to the majority what they are able to own and do.

> A man is none the less a slave because he is allowed
> to choose a new master once in a term of years.
>
> Lysander Spooner,
> American philosopher, 1870

In a genuinely free society, in order to get another person to do something you have to use persuasion, and have them agree voluntarily. The opposite is slavery, which remains today in various forms. Forced military service is temporary slavery, unless the person is killed in battle, in which case it is permanent. If something is worth fighting for, people will voluntarily fight; we do not need to be enslaved. This is a denial of our self-ownership.

> The real injustice of the draft is that it is state control
> over the individual - it's forced labor. Conscription
> as a means to any end is unjust. I'm not a pacifist
> resisting war - I'm a free man resisting slavery... I
> don't think it's wise to go to prison for my beliefs.
> After all, prison is equivalent to the draft. They're
> both slavery. They're both unjust and brutal. I've
> proudly broken the law, and I see going to court as a
> step to going to prison, just as I see registration as a
> big step to being drafted. I don't want to pretend

there's any legitimacy in a judge who wears black robes and was appointed by politicians who have made these unjust laws. I don't think he has any right to judge me or sentence me to prison. I don't need him to tell me that I'm innocent or right - I know those things already - and I sure don't want him to tell me I'm wrong and sentence me to jail.

Paul Jacob,
U.S. draft resister, 1983

How Government Complicates Rights

Government is a collection of individuals with the perceived legitimacy to initiate force within a given territory, which means they have the power to create laws which will give some people state-mandated entitlements, while denying other people their property rights and ultimately, they have the authority to enforce these laws at gunpoint. This is a system of forced redistribution of wealth. Going back to the library scenario, if the politicians or the majority of voters (depending on what kind of vote it is) agree that it is their right to have publicly funded libraries, then those people will be gaining their preference for a library while many others will be losing control over their own property – in this case the money that they have to pay in taxes. Essentially, government interferes with self-ownership and property rights by forcing some people to pay for other people's preferences.

It is true that liberty is precious - so precious that it must be rationed.

Vladimir Lenin,
Russian Marxist revolutionary, 1939

The power a multiple millionaire, who may be my neighbor and perhaps my employer, has over me is very much less than that which the smallest

33

> bureaucrat possesses who wields the coercive power
> of the state, and on whose discretion it depends
> whether and how I am to be allowed to live or work.
>
> Friedrich A. Hayek,
> Austrian economist, 1944

> Criminals are a small minority in any age or country.
> And the harm they have done to mankind is
> infinitesimal when compared to the horrors - the
> bloodshed, the wars, the persecutions, the
> confiscations, the famines, the enslavements, the
> wholesale destruction - perpetrated by mankind's
> governments. Potentially, a government is the most
> dangerous threat to man's rights: it holds a legal
> monopoly on the use of physical force against
> legally disarmed victims.
>
> Ayn Rand,
> Philosopher and novelist, 1964

The veil of government legitimacy can be lifted with a few simple
questions. I will ask them here so you can think about them, and
then you can ask them of your friends and family, and maybe even
some politicians. Do you think legitimate government power is
derived from the people? Most people who believe in government
will say yes. Do individuals have the right to initiate force against
other individuals? Since most people are not violent the common
answer is that people do not have the right to initiate force against
others. If they don't have that right, can they delegate it to the
government? This is where you will start to notice people's minds
squirming. Many put people and government on two different
planes of existence, with opposite moral codes, but believe that the
government plane of aggression can still derive its authority from
the non-aggression plane of the individual. Can you delegate a
right you do not have? This helps to clarify the point addressed in

* what about the right (34)
to bear arms?

question three. These conversations will get heated and possibly uncomfortable rather quickly. But you have seen how straightforward it is to dismantle the legitimacy of government that many people hold.

All any of us alive today have known is one form of government or another, and our compassion has mostly been measured in terms of how many services we believe the government should provide to those in need. It is almost inconceivable for most people to even consider the possibility of self-governance, and voluntary care for those in need. I am asking that when reading this book you suspend your attachment to what we have known and allow me to guide you into an exploration of what I believe is not only possible, but essential to our future prosperity. I assure you that this vision is inspired by nothing more than my compassion and my hope, though I know it can sound elitist and arrogant until you follow through with the analysis I offer.

RIGHTS AND THE ENVIRONMENT

The purpose of this section is to bring together environmentalists with non-environmentalists. I was once an ardent environmentalist, but as I learned the principles that I am now writing about, I came to the realization that there was a peaceful way to resolve our issues, and get our needs met. If people care about the natural environment they often call themselves "environmentalists", but there are some fundamental differences between environmentalists, who believe that nature has intrinsic value, and rights respecting individuals, who may value the environment but not above humans. I greatly appreciate many aspects of the natural environment and want them to be preserved by nonviolent methods. In other words, by understanding, and respecting, property rights.

The environmental movement is based on the belief that nature has intrinsic value. This includes mountains, marshes, streams, grasses, tadpoles, birds, cougars, snakes and millions more. Because each of these have intrinsic value, it follows that when people alter their environment for the betterment of humanity, by building houses, farms, cars, computers, clothes, etc., we are destroying that which has inherent value.

If a bear eats salmon, which eats smaller fish, which eat zooplankton, which feed off other plankton, which consumes phytoplankton, which live off chemicals in the water and sunlight, then which rights should we protect? The idea that everything in nature has intrinsic value merely acts to negate human values, because we cannot do anything without altering the environment.

An important distinction for me came when I would try to define what the environment was. It never sat well with me that definitions of nature and environment would almost always exclude humans and what we have produced. Reality is not so distinct, however. All of our creations are simply chemical rearrangements of what was already on this planet. In the same way that fish cannot live out of water, humans cannot be divorced from nature. If instead of viewing the environment as something distinct from humans, where every action we take destroys something with intrinsic value, we view it as our surroundings, suddenly the wonderful creations of humanity become part of our environment, and it can be seen that the reason we manipulate the naturally occurring elements is to enrich people's lives. When viewed in this light, it becomes apparent that the purpose of economic activity is to actually improve our environment.

Most people that are a part of the so-called environmental movement are caring people who are trying to do what they think is good. I do not believe that most of these caring individuals have

Oxford scholar - Gambrich?

thought about the implications of holding the belief that the natural environment has intrinsic value and therefore rights of its own. Once it is revealed that this worldview is both anti-human rights and impossible to live in accordance with consistently, the nonviolent option, which is based on property rights, will become more alluring. Why is it anti-human rights? Because if nature has intrinsic value, then everything we do which sustains our life destroys somethings with value. In order to survive we would have to assert our right over that which already has an intrinsic right.

While the Industrial Revolution has greatly improved the standard of living for those in relatively free market countries, the environmental movement is having the effect of lowering the standard of living for millions by not allowing people to use their own property as they choose. An improving standard of living is when more people are able to have more of their needs and desires met in an ethical way, whether they be material or non-material. A lower standard of living, on the other hand, would be when fewer of people's needs and desires are able to be met in ethical ways. When people are not able to use their property in ways which most meet the needs of themselves and the consumers, the result is fewer products and services offered which people would want. This means that the standard of living is lower than what it would be if people had full control of their property.

Some environmental policies are also artificially reducing the supply of energy and therefore increasing its price because of bans or restrictions on several kinds of energy production in the U.S. This acts to make very wealthy those who control oil in other countries. Further promotion of alternative energy sources in the form of subsidies as well as increased restrictions, regulations and taxes on traditional energy sources will lead to a significantly lower standard of living. In the free market, if alternative sources of energy could be produced more cost-effectively than traditional sources, then people and industries will naturally shift to the new sources. Energy is one of the key commodities which allow an economy to grow, and artificial increases in prices will inevitably reduce production.

While many environmentalists are concerned that human activity is destroying the environment, it is the products of the Industrial Revolution which allow us to more fully appreciate nature. We now have the capability to travel around the world, up into the stratosphere, and down under water, making use of roads, planes, cars, boats, submarines, and much, much more.

This has been an especially challenging lesson for me to learn, repeatedly having to let go of previously held beliefs in the face of overwhelming logic and evidence. I care deeply about the natural environment, and the fact that there has been much damage to it is unarguable. But why has there been so much destruction? Is it just that these capitalists don't care at all, and so they will destroy one resource after another until the whole planet has been ravaged? That is certainly what I thought.

But let's take a look at this situation through the lens of property rights. It is my contention that the understanding and enforcement of property rights will dramatically reduce the amount of environmental destruction and pollution, and will simultaneously lead to greater prosperity for everyone.

The only way humans, or any creature for that matter, can survive is to somehow alter the environment. So change to the environment is inevitable. When someone owns property, however, they tend to take care of it so that it will be sustainable in the long run so they can continue making a profit. When the resource is public, then the private companies who have access to the property face the *tragedy of the commons* problem, first described by Garret Hardin. When no one owns the resource, it is in each person's self-interest to use it as much as possible, because when they are not using it, other people are. In this way resources that are not privately owned are much more likely to be used up.

> The problem that the tragedy of the commons forces us to confront is, in fact, the core issue of political philosophy: how to protect or advance the interests of the collective as a whole when the individuals that make it up...behave in a selfish, greedy and quarrelsome fashion. The only answer is a sufficient measure of coercion.
>
> William Ophuls,
> American environmentalist, 1974

An example of *the tragedy of the commons* is logging on public lands. The government, which claims ownership of the land, sees that they could get some revenue by allowing some logging companies to take out some lumber for a limited time. These companies go in and cut down all of the trees within the allocated region, and have no incentive to replant because it is not their land, and they may not be able to profit in the future from the time, labor and resources they would be spending replanting the trees. Logging companies which spent these resources in the present would merely be giving charity to the companies with logging permissions in the future. The forestry policy of the U.S. has led to the destruction of large areas of timber lands, which led to mud slides, slumps, sloughs, earth flows, soil erosion and river silting (Anderson, 1990).

Aside from the government's own detrimental impact on the environment, it makes policies which subsidize the private sector to do the same: logging roads built at the government's expense and grazing permissions sold to ranchers at far below market cost make it cheaper for companies to use the resources, all while not having incentive for their practices to be sustainable. The companies don't have to pay the full cost, and the government certainly doesn't either, which means the cost of the destruction is paid for by us, the tax-payers.

In the Brazilian forests, an area many call the lungs of the planet, there is rapid deforestation. A study by the World Resource Institute found that cattle ranching and settlements by small farmers were the main culprits (Rehmke, 1989). This was made possible by the Brazilian government, which, by giving virtually free money in the form of subsidies, invited investors to purchase and cut down large areas of forest, turning them into farmland.

When a company owns a forest, without government intervention, they are constantly cutting and replanting, looking out for long-run sustainability. As long as the land was justly acquired, the owners should be able to do with it as they please. This does not mean that all wild lands will be used for logging, mining, oil drilling, etc. The owners will see what use people most value by seeing who will pay the most for it. If a timber company can get $1 million a year by chopping down the trees in a given area and replanting them, or it can get $2 million by turning it into a park, the choice they will make is obvious. In this way, the lands will go to their most desired use, even if that means staying exactly as they are. People have the opportunity to vote with their money. The Nature Conservancy is an organization that purchases land, with money from donations, to keep in its natural state. No need for coercion.

When someone has the desire for a land to stay natural, that is fine, but as soon as they use force, or the threat of force, they have crossed the line of property rights, and their actions are no longer just. Examples of force would be getting a law passed saying that the owner can no longer use his land, trespassing and spiking trees, or just refusing to get out of one of their trees. Peaceful resolutions would be purchasing the land or using persuasion to alter the owner's course of action.

It is clear that private owners will care for their land, and have a great incentive to make it sustainable, but what if there is a chemical plant next door to me, and it is spewing toxins onto my house? This is a key point here, which has been ignored since the mid-1800s in the United States, when the courts decided that industry had rights over people's private property because they were providing a "public good". The chemical plant is clearly violating your property rights, and you have the right to protect your property and get an injunction for them to stop their practices. The chemical company now has an incentive to internalize their pollution so they can continue in business. There are several options in this situation: the chemical company can stop business, they can pay you for the right to pollute a certain amount over a given timeframe, they can come up with a technology so their pollutants will not go outside in the first place, or they can just buy your land outright, with your consent. By this strict enforcement of property rights, all of a sudden the many negative externalities that environmentalists complain about will be internalized.

THE UNITED NATIONS, PROPERTY RIGHTS AND THE ENVIRONMENT

Rather than follow the principles of private property protection, those in the United Nations often choose to act in accordance with the ideologies of people like Marx, Mao, Lenin and Stalin.

The Conference Report from the 1976 United Nations Conference on Human Settlements, called "Habitat I", declares in its preamble:

> Land... cannot be treated as an ordinary asset, controlled by individuals subject to the pressures and the inefficiencies of the market. Private land ownership is also a principle instrument of accumulation and concentration of wealth and therefore contributes to social injustice... Public control of land use is therefore indispensable. (Jasper, 2001)

In the main body of the text, the following socialist policies are proposed:

> Recommendation D.1 Land Resource Management
> (a) Public ownership or effective control of land in the public interest is the single most important means of ... achieving a more equitable distribution of the benefits of development whilst assuring that environmental impacts are considered.
> (b) Land is a scarce resource whose management should be subject to public surveillance or control in the interest of the nation...
> (d) ...Governments must maintain full jurisdiction and exercise complete sovereignty over such land with a view to freely planning human settlements.

The result of the 1992 UN Earth summit was a document called Agenda 21, which sought to micromanage every square inch of the planet. It claimed that "land must be regarded primarily as a set of essential terrestrial ecosystems and only secondly as a source of resources." The idea is to take rights away from the individual and give it to ever growing bureaucracies. It states that, "All countries should also develop national land-management plans to guide development." (Jasper, 2001)

Many people believe that the United Nations is merely a goodwill organization with no real power. Being aware that most people, particularly in the United States would be opposed to world government, the United Nations has taken the slow but steady approach, starting off as just a paper organization and growing to have a military, the authority to decide who and what has rights and what they are, and nearing the ability to tax globally. In the years to come, there will most likely be calls for them to enforce the dictates in their documents more steadfastly. While most people have either no knowledge of the UN or just hold the idea that they are a benevolent organization, the purpose here is to show their true philosophy and how it contradicts the logic of property rights that we have set forth.

Along with Agenda 21, The Global Biodiversity Assessment (GBA) emerged from the 1992 Rio Earth Summit. This 1,140-page document claims that "property rights are not absolute and unchanging, but rather a complex, dynamic and shifting relationship between two or more parties over space and time." (Jasper, 2001) This is basically the same philosophy that Karl Marx espoused, taking the rights away from the individual and giving them to an elite group of people to decide for the rest.

The GBA states further that "we should accept biodiversity [e.g., plants and animals] as a legal subject, and supply it with adequate rights." This means that the same rights we have would be assigned to animals, insects, trees, bushes, marshes and mountains, and that "guardians" would then be appointed to protect these rights. Rather than being able to do as you please with your own property, the GBA states that "it would therefore become necessary to justify any interference with biodiversity, and to provide proof that human interests justify damage caused to biodiversity." (Jasper, 2001) As was shown earlier in this chapter, the only way that any species can survive is by manipulating its environment, but under this scenario the "guardian" who represents the plants, insects or trees can claim "rights" which supersede the rights of the actual property owner.

PROPERTY RIGHTS AND THIRD WORLD POVERTY

Why are so many people in Third World countries continuously in poverty? Many think capitalism has destroyed those economies and that lack of money is the major problem. Money, in the form of investments, can definitely help, but not until some other pieces are sorted out first. The primary reason that they are not able to have economic growth like the industrialized regions is the lack of sufficient property rights protection and too many bureaucratic barriers to start and be successful in business.

Economist Hernando de Soto and his team tried to set up a business in the U.S. and in Lima, Peru. Working 6-hour days, they were able to set up the American-based business in one day, while the Lima-based business took 289 days and cost 31-times the average monthly wage. This sort of red-tape prevents many people from starting and growing a business. The property that they do own is not very well protected legally, so they do not have incentive to expand and thrive. Why would someone want to invest a lot of time and money in growing a business if they weren't sure they would be allowed to operate the next day? (Soto, 2000)

There are plenty of resources in Third World countries, and plenty of people who want to improve their condition. What they need is an understanding and respect for private property and then you will see them catching up to the First World countries rather quickly in their abilities to meet people's needs and desires, whether material or non-material. It is not capitalism which leaves many destitute but rather lack of access to participate in capitalism. When private companies make deals with governments to take possession of the people's land, or when the people's resources must be given up in payment of loans that the governments have taken out, capitalism is being sharply violated.

EMINENT DOMAIN

Eminent domain is a claim that the government makes on your property in order to take it from you without your permission. This commonly occurs when the government wants to build highways or railroads or condemn "blighted" homes or neighborhoods. They claim the person's property is in the way, pay them what they believe is fair, and kick out the owners.

These days things have gone even further with city councils giving homeowners the boot in order to give the property to private developers. These developers demolish the existing building and erect something more upscale. The government usually takes these actions because they hope to get greater tax revenue from the new development.

But wait. Hold on a minute.

As was laid out earlier, rights cannot be aggregated. The city council, or any other group of people do not have any right to take away another person's property. Any claim of eminent domain is unjust. It is often allowed to go through on the argument that the new development will stimulate the economy. But is this true? Unfortunately, this a typically short-sighted perspective of governments, whether small or large. Yes, a development can enrich a community, but only by taking away from other places. If subsidies allow more jobs to come to your city and more homes to be built, they are at the cost of other cities which lose those people and products.

In 2000, hoping to revitalize their community and increase tax revenue, the local government of the City of New London, Connecticut, came up with a redevelopment plan. The city government-controlled development company offered to purchase all 115 residential and commercial lots which were located where they wanted to build. However, 15 of the owners did not want to sell. Even though the residences were not "blighted", the City of New London decided to exercise its power of eminent domain and forcefully evict the stubborn owners. Nine of the owners banded together, led by Susette Kelo, and took the case to the highest courts in America.

On June 23, 2005, the United States Supreme Court made a decision in favor of the City of New London, allowing them to take property from residents and give it to private developers. This decision opened the floodgates to governments taking non-blighted property in order to increase tax revenues, thereby degrading our property rights even further. (Institute for Justice, 2009)

There are always nonviolent solutions to these scenarios where eminent domain is invoked. If you want to build a road, figure out multiple route options in case some people are not willing to sell their homes. If a home is in poor condition, often called "blighted", and is not a part of a housing community with building upkeep requirements, then the person must be left alone. A developer can either offer a high enough amount to get the people to sell, or alter the size or location of the development.

Most people think that if they purchased and paid off their home that they own it. In a free market this would be true, but under our current system you still do not have ultimate control over your property. You will see very quickly who controls your property if you decide to no longer pay your taxes on it.

This is a simple issue really. When these cases are brought to court, they are made to sound very complex. But it comes down to owning one's property. That's it. In a free society, other people cannot legitimately use coercion to take your property from you, even if there are many of them.

What you own justly, you have total control over. If someone tries to take your property against your will, they are acting unethically.

A Country versus A Country Club

Many people argue that living in a country is like being a member of a country club or homeowner's association and that if we do not like the club we can leave. Taxes are like dues, and government regulation is like a club's terms-of-use contract. In each case you must pay, but you get many benefits in return.

So if I am unhappy with the government taking my property and having most of my life regulated should I just leave and look for a less oppressive country? This is a common response I get when discussing the immorality of government. But saying that if you don't like it here you can leave is a very simplistic approach that fails to look at the key distinctions between a country and a country club.

The first distinction is in property acquisition. A country club gets property by way of voluntary exchange or being the first to develop on it. Let's say some people want to build a tennis club. If it is land with no owner that they seek, they will probably be looking in a fairly desolate location and can claim ownership by being the first to develop. If they are seeking to be in an area with more people, they will probably have to purchase the space from someone. Either way the property was acquired justly.

How does a country go about getting its real estate? One way is for the government to forcibly remove those who are in the areas it wants to be. Another is for the government to claim vast areas as its own without any sort of land manipulation. Therefore anyone who decides to homestead in that area is on the government's land and must abide by its rules. You may be thinking that the government can also pay for land that was previously owned, and thereby become the just owners. The problem is how they can afford the property. This, of course, is paid for through taxes because governments are not productive themselves. So the only way they can acquire land is by forcing other people to pay for it.

The second key distinction is between taxes and dues, which builds upon the first distinction. People join clubs because they weigh the benefits and the costs and decide that they would prefer being a member versus keeping money or spending it on something else. If someone does not think that they are getting their money's worth, they can terminate membership and look elsewhere for a better club or forego a club altogether. On the other hand, if you reside in a place the government claims is within their boundaries, then they will force you to pay taxes, whether or not you believe that what you are getting in return is of greater value.

Many claim that there is a social contract between the government and the people in which the people give up certain rights for the "public good". Because we are born within certain geographical boundaries which the government claims, it is our "duty" to give this government much of our time, money and energy, for the duration of our lives within those boundaries. It is important to note that there is no such contract. A contract binds those parties which sign the document. I don't know of anyone who has signed a contract with the government, completely voluntarily, which gives the government the authority to ultimately control one's property.

As you can see, it really comes down to the acquisition of property. If you become the owner in a just way, then you can set the terms if others want to take residence on your land. They will get to weigh the pros and cons and choose what they believe is best. If you unjustly claim ownership of land, then all of the subsequent taxes and regulations will also be unjust.

It is important to see that the institution of government should not have any special rights above the ordinary person. Since rights cannot be aggregated to have power over the minority - or the smallest minority, the individual - it becomes apparent that government is not some superhuman organization but simply a group of people who are asserting their will over others. The actions of governments are always unethical because they only exist, to the degree which they do, by violating people's property rights.

I OBJECT!
ANSWERS TO COMMON QUESTIONS AND OBJECTIONS

Property is theft. No one can own property!
In order to raise this objection, one must have control, or ownership, of one's faculties. So one inherently owns one's body, whether or not that is always respected. For property outside of our bodies, were we not to put to use natural resources, we would all die rather quickly. For me to eat a banana off of a tree, I am claiming ownership of it. Nobody else can eat what I have just consumed. To put it another way, either no one can control property or everyone can. Since people can and need to in order to survive, then property rights are valid for everyone.

We do not own the land. We are borrowing, or even stealing it from future generations.
This has some emotional pull to it because most parents do care about their children, and want their children to be able to have better lives than they have. However, there are some fatal flaws in this perspective. First, you cannot borrow or steal from that which does not exist. Since future generations do not presently exist, nothing can be taken from them. Second, the only way we have been able to raise our standard of living has been by utilizing resources in ever more productive ways. If people 1000 years ago had foregone the use of resources beyond what was needed just to survive in order to conserve for our present generation, we would all be living in poverty. Because people did not stop using resources, they were able to accumulate capital and build machines which could produce goods more efficiently as well as find and take advantage of even more resources, all for the purpose of bettering human life. The same is true now - if we forego the use of resources in order to conserve, we are effectively lowering our standard of living, as well as for future generations because they will not be able to benefit from our increased productivity.

Arguments such as this are essentially promoting socialism - having centralized government control over resources. People are prohibited from making free, nonviolent choices and having control over their property because it is believed that the results will be a worse planet for our descendants.

A truly free market, rather than condemning future generations to live off the remains of a consumption culture, allows each generation to attain a higher standard of living than the one before. When the logic and morality of the free market finally sway the masses, it will not take long for people's material lives to be far beyond what we can even imagine now. By utilizing our resources, accumulating capital and increasing our productivity we are bequeathing to future generations a much higher standard of living. We do not need to forego consumption to supposedly benefit those who will already be far better off than we are today.

Native Americans survived just fine without property rights.

The story has been told many times, that the Native Americans were naturally collectivist, and that they did not believe in property rights. Until recently, I had just taken this as the truth, but is it? To the contrary, I found that the vast majority of tribes held strict property rights laws, not only protecting one tribe's land from another, but also protecting the individual property from other individuals. For example, when hunting buffalo, the arrows would have an identifying mark, so that the person who shot the arrow which killed the animal could be rewarded with the choicest cuts (Anderson, 1996). Also, a number of salmon streams were privately owned, resulting in better husbandry (Johnson, 2006).

So why is the common perception of Natives so different from reality? Well, there are two primary reasons: first, when settlers were pushing West, they came across a nomadic tribe, which did not place much value in specific pieces of land. When word of this got back to the East Coast newspapers, they repeated this experience as though all Natives had the same perspectives. Over time this was just assumed to be true without actually looking at reality. Second, most modern tribes are thought of as collectivist because they have been forced onto reservations, where they do not actually own the land – it is held in trust by the federal government.

On land that was not privately owned, the Native Americans faced the same *tragedy of the commons* that we face today. Studies show that many bird species were in decline or had gone extinct due to over-hunting, and the same goes for the buffalo. Even before the Europeans began killing the buffalo, they were already being systematically over-hunted as tribes would compete with one another for territory. (Benson, 2006)

The poverty that many Native Americans currently face is largely due to the structure of property rights and the rule of law (Anderson, 2006). Today there are three kinds of land ownership for Native Americans: privately owned property (fee simple), property held in trust by the Federal Government but allotted to tribal members (individual trust), and land for a tribe held in trust by the government (tribal trust). The last two types of ownership have complex bureaucracies which oversee what occurs on the land. So which type of ownership do you think yields the most productivity on the land? Researchers Terry Anderson and Dean Lueck found that individual trust lands were 30 to 40 percent less productive and tribal trust lands were 80 to 90 percent less productive than fee simple lands (Anderson et al., 1992).

The Native Americans need to be able to own the land outright, so they can do with it what they choose. No more forced land collectivism. Their level of prosperity will greatly rise if they can make use of their property rights and have them protected.

What about the rights of nature and species?

Private property ownership brings up concerns for some people about the well being of non-human life as well as ecosystems and mountains. It does not seem right to some people that we are the only being which have rights. It is claimed that animals, insects, trees, grasses, mountains and water have rights of their own. I sympathize with feeling a great connection with the natural world, and its remarkable beauty. Ultimately, each organism on the planet has to alter its environment in order to survive, and if everything had equal rights, then nothing would be allowed to survive.

It is impossible to hold consistently the belief that everything in nature has rights. People who claim this often drive cars or ride bikes, eat food, live in a house and wear clothes. All of these activities manipulate the environment and assert one's right to property and life over that which was used in the creation of the product as well as that which was displaced by the use of the products (e.g., roads, houses, factories, and stores take up space that other creatures can no longer occupy).

Fortunately, far from private property being the end of the natural world, it is the path to ethically preserve natural land which people highly value in that form. People are able to pool their resources to acquire land to protect it and its non-human occupants.

How You Will Benefit from Adherence to Property Rights

Now that the fundamentals of self-ownership and property rights have been laid out, it should be apparent that you would personally be much better off if you actually got to keep what was yours and were able to dispose of your property as you saw fit. This society of voluntary exchange will lead to greater prosperity for nearly everyone through nonviolent means. Just imagine: All of the money that you earn is yours, and you get to do exactly what you want with it. As long as you don't initiate aggression against others, the world is wide open to you.

> Thinkers and writers who would deny property rights or create political rights over private property, are the ultimate heralds and harbingers of dictatorships.
>
> Hans F. Sennholz,
> German economist, 1982

The Secrets to Nonviolent Prosperity

54

Chapter 3

MONEY MADNESS

In 2007, the United States government raided the facilities of Liberty Dollar, a company which independently produced their own money, 100% backed by silver and gold. People could purchase this money and voluntarily exchange it with those local merchants who would accept it. Over the previous decade, more and more people had been seeing the value in commodity-based money, which is money that either is a good or is backed by a good, such as gold and silver. Thus there came to be over $20 million worth of this independent currency in circulation. Though the government had previously stated on many occasions that they had no problem with the alternative money, and that it was completely legitimate, they went ahead and seized all of the precious metals in the warehouse as well as all of the company records. After all of this time, they claimed that the Liberty Dollar looked too similar to Federal Reserve currency and was therefore counterfeit. Many do not know that creating or using private currencies is completely legitimate, and that the primary reason they are not more popular is because one cannot pay taxes with these alternative currencies.

The government's money no longer contains or is backed by any precious metals. Nowadays when the government makes copies of its money, whether in digital or paper form, it is they who are in fact producing counterfeit money. This is an age-old battle between those who want value-based money versus those who benefit from using fiat currency, which is money issued by the state, without any commodity backing.

> An International Monetary Fund seminar of eminent economists couldn't agree on what money is and how banks create it.
>
> *Wall Street Journal*,
> September 24, 1971

Many people are in a panic over the rapidly depreciating dollar. They are seeing their hard work, and a lifetime of saving losing value quickly. Increasing numbers are helpless, and hopeless, not sure of what steps to take to protect their assets. What is going on with the monetary system?

Now that we have explored the issue of private property and its direct relationship to prosperity, we now turn to the wonderful, yet often mysterious topic of money. It's something that people want more of, but do not know much about. I have always liked money, and have enjoyed collecting currencies from various countries, but I did not really know what was taking temporary residence in my wallet. I didn't even know that I didn't know much about it. The contents of this section may be quite shocking if you are unfamiliar with the nature of money and the current status of commonly used currency.

No matter how people get their money - whether they worked for, inherited, or won it in a lottery - there are very core level emotions related to our survival and our success that we associate with it. There are so many questions that everybody has about money: What is money? Who makes it? Who controls it? How does it function in the economy? How do we know if there is enough of it? Did governments invent money? Okay, maybe not everybody has these questions; maybe only a few have thought to ask. But now that I have written the questions down and they are staring you in the face, I will count you among those who have asked.

Before we get further into this topic, let's take a moment to answer these first questions. Money is a medium of exchange, and can really be any object that is regularly used for payments. These days, nearly all money is created by central banks because they have a government enforced monopoly to create the currency that people need to pay taxes. The dominant currency is that which is needed to pay taxes. This doesn't mean that only governments and central banks can create money. Anybody can come up with previously existing or newly created commodities which they can use as a medium of exchange.

The same people who create the money, control its supply and therefore its value. In a free market, a company producing a medium of exchange would not have any significant control over its value once it is in the market. Central banks and governments are different though because they can manipulate the interest rate, which directly effects the supply of money and its value. As you will see in this chapter, money arose organically among people like language.

The supply of money is regulated by central banks and governments, but does it need to be? Money is like any other commodity in a free market, where supply and demand will lead to the proper amount being available. Money is different than other commodities in one major way though. Generally an increased number of some commodity leads to a societal benefit, but not so with a medium of exchange because that just leads to inflation, or a devaluation of the money. That is to say that the appropriate amount of money in a society would best be left to the free market, which can adapt more quickly to supply and demand than can a government. But I am getting ahead of myself. So let's get back to the basics.

Why should you care about this issue? As you will see, there is tremendous power in controlling the currency for a population, especially when the money being used is fiat, and does not have any free market value. Let's keep in mind the importance of private property that we established as we delve into the issue of money.

THE NATURE OF MONEY

First we must look at why people exchange in the first place. This takes place because each person engaging in the trade believes that he will be better off after the trade than before. Whether or not that belief holds true after the exchange is made is irrelevant; it is the belief that he will prefer the new situation. Let's take a look at the development of satisfying one's needs, from being self-sufficient, through direct and indirect exchange, and to the natural arising of money.

Self-Sufficiency

If I am completely self-sufficient on a piece of land, then I have no need for money because there is nothing outside of my property that I want. I consume the goods directly.

Barter

Now imagine that I have a neighbor who makes delicious pies. I approach her and ask if I can have one, and she agrees to give me a pie in exchange for a hat that I made. This direct exchange of goods is called barter. While this has expanded the number of items I can get, there are very severe limits to production because every time you want something, you have to find something that you have that you are willing to give away. There are also problems when what you are willing to give away is not easily divisible. For example, if you have a piano, and you want some lettuce, you will not just take off one key to trade for the head of lettuce.

Indirect Exchange

A more efficient way to exchange is indirectly. How does this work? Say I have a watermelon, and I want to trade it for some cookies. I find someone who has cookies and is willing to trade, but not for watermelon. He wants ice cream. Fortunately I know a guy who is willing to trade some ice cream for my watermelon. I then rush over to the baker and trade my ice cream for his cookies. Thus each person gets what they wanted, and more desires have been satisfied than with direct barter. While there are more possibilities for exchange with indirect versus direct barter, some of the same obstacles are still present, such as the coincidence of wants. You always have to find someone who is willing to accept your product or service, which can be a challenge if your work is highly specialized or your product is not easily divisible.

How Money Arises

Pretty soon the demand will increase for the commodity most commonly accepted in exchange. People will use these items more often for the purpose of exchange rather than for consumption. The most popular of these different commodities comes to be known as *media for exchange*, also known as *money*. Many different goods have been used throughout history, such as tobacco, salt, cattle, nails, sugar, copper, grain, breads, tea, cowry shells and fishhooks. For several reasons, the two commodities that have endured the test of time more than any other are silver and gold: they have many uses aside from money, they are easily divisible (as opposed to jewels), and they are durable (as opposed to sugar). Through the process of the free market, a commodity will come to be used as money. Rather than being the root of all evil, the existence of money makes possible our modern material society.

INFLATION

Inflation is something unnatural to the free market, and always leads to catastrophe, whether slowly through a subtle leaching of value or the rapid drop in value that comes from hyperinflation. This theft of people's purchasing power is directed through a policy of increasing the money supply. Prices of goods rise because of inflation, but that is not inflation itself. Economist Murray Rothbard defined inflation as an increase in the supply of money in an economic system greater than the increase in precious metals.

> Conferences on inflation are customarily attended by the politicians who caused it and the economists who showed them how.
>
> Richard Needham,
> English politician, 1977

CASE STUDY: *The Fall of Rome*

After Caesar was murdered in 44 BC, his adopted son Octavian took power, bringing an end to years of war and fostering an era of peace. He greatly increased economic freedom by lowering the tax burden and encouraging private enterprise, free trade and private land ownership, leading to a time of greater prosperity for the Romans. Unfortunately, the Roman Empire did not follow this path in the long run, and a combination of subsidies, heavy taxation, inflation and over-regulation led to its fall.

In order to keep power, the emperors purposefully overtaxed the wealthy, making them powerless. Once the formerly wealthy had been taxed-out and could no longer pay the costs of government work programs, the burden fell to the middle and lower classes. Debasement of commodity-money was their form of inflation. This is done by mixing a cheaper metal in with the more valuable metal the coin consists of, while keeping its face value the same. By 268

A.D., the amount in a supposedly 100% silver denarius was just 0.02%. Inflation combined with high taxes destroyed capital accumulation, therefore crippling the economy, and forcing them to resort to barter. Decreased production led to dramatically lower revenues for the State, which then could not fund its basic functions. This allowed for them to be taken over by other empires.

FRACTIONAL-RESERVE BANKING

Aside from making coins, goldsmiths became storage facilities because people did not want to be carrying around all of their money with them, or have it stolen from their homes. The goldsmith would give his customers a paper receipt for the gold stored in his safe. Because these paper receipts were a lot lighter, and therefore more convenient, people began using the warehouse receipts as money instead of the gold itself. They were trading over the title to the gold. If someone wanted the actual gold, they would just go to the goldsmith, hand him the receipt and get the gold in return. As people became more confident that the piece of paper would be converted into gold, the metal itself was used less and less often, and the paper receipts became the primary medium of exchange.

The customers were not the only ones who appreciated this; the goldsmiths, now known as bankers, were able to charge a storage fee for the gold that they held secure. But they had other ideas, more sinister. They realized that only rarely would someone come to claim the gold, so they decided to write more warehouse receipts than there was gold and loan them out.

To make this important point clear, it is as if auto manufacturers printed out more car titles than they manufactured cars, and sold the car titles on the market as if they were really titles to cars. So not everybody who paid full value for a car title has a car to drive.

Hence we arrive at the term *fractional-reserve banking*, because the receipts are no longer backed up 100% by metal or another commodity; it is only a fraction of that. What would happen if everyone with a receipt went to the bank and requested the amount of gold noted on the paper? That amount does not exist and so the bank would close to prevent people from trying to extract their money, as has happened many times in banking history. Fractional-reserve banking is fraudulent because the customer does not actually have a guarantee to the gold money as the warehouse receipt declares.

In fractional-reserve banking, the fraction is how much the bank has to keep in reserve (in the vaults) compared to how many claims for the money in reserve they can loan out. Let's say that the reserve was 100%. That would mean that every dollar loaned out was completely backed by gold. What if the reserve was 50%? Then for every ounce of gold in the vaults, there would be claims for two-ounces loaned out. All of a sudden, only half the amount shown on the bill or bank account can actually be redeemed in real gold from the vaults.

What would happen if the reserve were lowered to 10%? This would mean that for every $10 loaned out, $1 would have to actually be redeemable in gold, the rest claim to be backed by something but in reality are not. It is not as if there are some special bills which could be redeemed, it is just that only 10% of the claims at any given time could be redeemed because that is all of the gold that exists in the vaults. For the big banks, the reserve ratio has been lowered down to 3.33%. So if one of these banks had $1 worth of gold in their vault, how much would they be able to loan out? Since the ratio is 33 to 1, for every dollar in the vault, they would be able to loan out $33 in claims to that dollar. Something starting to seem fishy to you?

The gold standard of the late 1800's was not 100% backed, but fractional-reserve, thus still causing periods of inflation followed by periods of deflation, which led to depression. Deflation would set in when banks became concerned about their gold reserves and would stop the expansion of their notes. This tight credit would result in many business failures which would lead to banks failing. Failing banks lead to depressions because there is a sudden reduction in the money supply. The reduced supply of money decreases the amount of spending, which lowers business earnings and consumer's earnings. The problems continue until prices and wages can lower to their market level in accordance with the new, decreased quantity of money. This sort of economic contraction is just what happened in 2008.

All modern banking is fractional-reserve, with reserve ratios at around 10-percent, and many of the big banks even lower at around 3-percent. Even the ratio of 10% is deceptive though, because that reserve money is not a commodity, like a precious metal, but merely fabricated fiat currency. Therefore, all banks are committing fraud on their customers. Once it was discovered that lenders were committing this sort of fraud, rather than the government barring this unjust activity, putting the scoundrels in jail and making them pay retribution, the government decided to get in on the action and institutionalize the practice.

PAPER CURRENCY

After awhile, people forgot where the value of warehouse receipts came from (i.e., the gold and silver), and they treated the pieces of paper as the thing of value itself. This has several undesirable consequences. Primarily, a government will issue fiat money, which is paper money with no commodity backing. This idea of "money for nothing" may sound good at first, but with fiat money there is almost a guarantee of inflation. Throughout history when money has become fiat as opposed to being commodity-based, those who have the power to issue the pieces of paper have tended to abuse that power and go down the path of devaluing the money. This is why those who wish to control the money try to divorce it from a commodity backing.

A Brief History of Paper Money

The Chinese are credited with the invention of paper money with the "flying money" of the Tang Dynasty in 619. Marco Polo brought the story of paper money back to Europe and was amazed that by simply putting a stamp on a piece of mulberry bark, the state could force people to accept it as money.

Kublai Khan used paper money in China in 1273 as he ruled one of the largest empires in history. He got people to use paper by outlawing gold and silver, giving out his paper money in payment, and forcing people to accept and use it under penalty of great punishment.

In 1661, the Stockholm Bank issued the first paper note as they were experiencing a shortage of coins. People appreciated the light weight of the paper compared to carrying around metal.

Desperate for money, the new English rulers, Williams III and Mary II, created the Bank of England with Scottish financier, William Patterson, in 1694, and were the first to institutionalize fractional-reserve paper money.

The Massachusetts Bay Colony printed the first paper currency in America around 1690. Benjamin Franklin, whom many consider the father of American paper currency, printed money his whole life. He was able to do what most politicians are not, which is simply to increase the supply of money as population increases in order to facilitate trade. Asked by the British Parliament why the colony was so prosperous, he shared with them about the debt-free paper money. This caused the British to outlaw their use of

Colonial Scrip, as it was called. The banning of their money is thought by many to be the deeper reason to what precipitated the Revolutionary War (NotHaus, 2003).

The Colonies financed the war by printing a seemingly endless stream of Continentals, issued by the Continental Congress. People could see that the Continentals were rapidly losing value due to their increasing supply, and their refusal to accept these nearly worthless pieces of paper led the Congress to make them legal tender, so people were forced to accept them.

While Franklin's integrity barred him from overprinting the paper money, the flaw in the system was exploited during the Revolutionary War, when the power to control the money supply lay in the hands of a few who chose to rapidly increase it, destroying people's savings and ruining the economy. This episode made the Founding Fathers aware of the dangers of fiat currency, and led them to incorporate language both in the Constitution and the Coin Act declaring money to be precious metals (i.e., silver), and specifically prohibiting baseless paper money. They did not want the power over the money system to be in a few hands. Unfortunately, we have strayed from their understanding.

In 1789, France found itself in serious debt and people were wondering what to do about it. Jacques Necker, The Minister of Finance, argued against the issuance of paper money as he was well aware of France's previous disastrous experience. But a speaker named Martineau stated to the Constituent Assembly, "Paper money under a despotism is dangerous, it favors corruption, but in a nation constitutionally governed the danger no longer exists." (White, 1896) He was able to sway the voters, and the new currency flooded France in successive waves. The "Reign of Terror" followed, with many merchants who were unwilling to accept the worthless paper currency being taken to the guillotine.

The economic collapse, due in part to the rapidly increasing money supply, left people calling for someone to lead them out of the mess. And thus Napoleon was able to rise to power.

It wasn't until 1973 that the U.S. dollar was completely fiat, meaning it had no commodity backing at all. Before 1933, each paper note was a claim to gold or silver. Starting in 1933, however, Americans were not allowed to get the gold in return for their paper notes, and they were even prohibited from owning gold. The dollar was not fully separated from gold though, as central banks and foreigners could still cash in their dollars for gold. This of course led the gold to flow out of the country, and primarily into the hands of central banks. 1973 is when the US said it would no longer redeem paper note claims for gold from anyone, even foreigners and central banks. The world thus entered the era we are currently in of fluctuating fiat currencies with nothing to keep inflation in check.

The proponents of paper money at the time believed that it was the dollar that was propping up the price of gold and not the other way around. Once the dollar was finally on its own, they believed, the price of gold would plummet down to around $8 per ounce. It was just in 1973 when the official US gold price was $42.22 - the amount for which the government would exchange one ounce of gold - and now the market price is over $1600.

DIGITAL CURRENCY

Fractional-reserve banking is very easy for the bankers to get away with in this day of digital currency. Only about 3% of our money is paper and coin, the rest just being numbers on computers. Why does intangible currency make it easier to inflate? Imagine you take a picture of a watch and email that picture to your friend. Now you each have a copy of that picture, increasing the number of pictures by 100%. Now imagine that you have a real watch that you give to your friend. You no longer have that watch. Things which are physical are not so easily multiplied - real work has to go into the production of a second watch.

The jig would be up very quickly if it were not just numbers that were deposited and loaned but real commodities. Then banks could only loan what actually existed and the customers could be sure that what they deposited would actually be there. Let's imagine silver was the primary currency used. People would deposit their silver at the bank to either be stored or loaned out. If it was stored, they would have immediate access to it. If it was to be loaned out, the bank would take the silver and loan it out. The recipient of the loan would get actual silver, not just numbers in an account on a computer. By using a commodity, each person who had numbers in their account would have actual money, not just claims to nonexistent money.

* * *

On a 100% gold or silver standard, the politically ambitious cannot simply grow the supply of money by stroke of a pen, and thus gold keeps inflation in check. This is exactly why those in government wanted to separate the paper from its commodity backing. When people use gold as money, the government cannot effectively control the supply, but if it is purely fiat, then they can print copies all day long. With gold, or any other commodity-based money that people choose, its value goes up and down *independent* of the will of the government. The value of fiat money, on the other hand, is directly related to the actions of the government.

The difference between commodity money and paper or digital money comes down to the rate at which the quantity can be increased. A precious metal, for example, must be extracted from the ground using very labor intensive means. Paper money can be produced at very little cost and digital currency can be produced at essentially no cost while their quantity is virtually limitless.

ARE WEALTH AND MONEY THE SAME?

Before getting too far, let me address a key misconception that many people have, that wealth and money are the same thing.

Wealth consists of the material goods that people make, such as houses, autos, steel mills, pipeline, factories, lumber and food, as well as land and natural resources in the ground in so far as people can use them. While people do not create natural resources, they do turn the resources into wealth by making them usable to people. Human beings turn chemical elements and other natural resources into desirable goods by our technological advances. All the oil and coal that is available to us today was available during the stone age, but it was not a good because they were not able to utilize it as we are today.

Wealth can increase while the money supply stays the same, the result of which is lower prices. On the flip side, if wealth stays the same or increases more slowly than does the money supply, prices go up and our purchasing power goes down. To illustrate why this is so, let's imagine we've got 1000 apples and $1000 dollars. The apples are the wealth and the dollars are the money supply. The average cost of an apple is $1. If there were still 1000 apples, but the supply of money doubled to $2000, would people be wealthier? No, they would simply pay twice as many dollars for the apple. The value of each dollar would have gone down by 50%. Now, if the supply of money stayed at $1000, but through better production methods the supply of apples increased to 2000, would people be wealthier? Yes, because there are more goods that they can purchase with the same amount of money. The average cost of an apple decreased by 50%, and so people became twice as wealthy. Hopefully it is more apparent now how wealth and the supply of money are independent.

It is important to note that all of the popular measures of the production of wealth, such as the Gross National Product (GNP) and the Gross Domestic Product (GDP), are fundamentally measures of the quantity of money and spending and not the quantity of goods produced. Their increase is caused by an increase in the supply of money and not necessarily an increase in the production of goods. Stocks, bonds and bank deposits are not wealth, but claims to wealth.

Q.T.O.M

A cool acronym is the best way I could think of to make the *quantity theory of money* sound exciting. As I will show, it is the only logical explanation of a sustained, economy-wide rise in prices. Very simply, the more money that exists, the more is spent, and this general increase in demand leads to a rise in prices.

Imagine awhile back when gold was used as money, when someone would discover gold, they would dig it out, melt it down into coins and spend it. The people who receive the new gold will then spend it as well, and on and on. This increase in the supply of gold leads to an increase in spending.

Let's say that you want to find the average price of a cup of coffee at the local cafe over the past week. Assume 1000 cups were sold, and $2000 was taken in. The average price for a cup of coffee would be $2. Now what could possibly lead to an increase in the average price? Well, there are only two options. One way is for the supply of coffee to decrease, which would mean that $2000 was going to be spent on, say, 500 cups of coffee, resulting in an average cost of $4. The other way is for the quantity of money to increase. If the quantity of money is doubled, so now people have $4000 to spend on 1000 cups of coffee, again the average price is $4. So the only two ways for sustained, economy-wide price increases are either a decrease in the supply of goods or an increase in the supply of money.

This is a critical concept to get in order to understand how inflation works, so we are going to go over it a bit more.

If there are 100 bananas (the quantity of the goods) and $100 to spend on bananas (the supply of money), what is the average price for a banana? (Answer: $1)

If there are still 100 bananas to buy, but now there are $110 to spend, what is the average price? (Answer: $1.10) The increased supply of money relative to the supply of goods resulted in higher prices.

If there are now $110 to spend and production has increased the supply of bananas to 220, what is the average price? (Answer: $0.50) The increase in the supply of goods relative to the supply of money resulted in a decease in the price of goods.

Let's say there are $100 to spend, but the supply of bananas has fallen to 25, what is the average price? (Answer: $4) A decrease in the supply of goods relative to the supply of money resulted in an increase in the price of goods.

If there are 100 bananas to buy but the supply of money has dropped to $50, what is the average price? (Answer: $0.50) A decrease in the supply of money relative to the supply of goods resulted in a decrease in prices.

While this may have seemed like a middle school pop-quiz, hopefully this has made it more clear that the only components which affect general price levels are the quantity of goods and the quantity of money. If the money supply increases faster than the supply of goods, then prices will do what? They will go up. And if the money supply drops while the supply of goods increases, stays the same or decreases less quickly than the supply of money, what will happen to prices? They will go down.

Without even needing to resort to specific numbers, do you think the supply of goods has increased or decreased during the past 100 years? The supply has most certainly increased substantially as we now have many more cars, houses, planes, computers, clothes, food, and pretty much everything else (except maybe horse-drawn carriages). If the supply has increased, then what explanation does that leave us for the vast increases in prices over the same time? You got it - the quantity of money in our economy has increased. If the spending had stayed the same over the past 100 years, meaning the quantity of money stayed the same, the prices would have gone down dramatically. This price reduction would result in greater purchasing power.

If we had just a 3% annual rise in prices over the course of the past century while the quantity of money stayed constant, the supply of goods would have to be reduced to less than 5% of what it was 100 years ago! [$1 \times 0.97^{100} = 4.76\%$] We now know that if the supply of money stays the same the only way for general prices to rise is for the supply of goods to decrease. According to economist George Reisman, "This would be a more rapid rate of economic decline than occurred during the collapse of the Roman Empire." (Reisman, 1976). We need to keep in mind that there are only two ways to increase general price levels: an increase in the supply of money and/or a decrease in the supply of goods.

If we say that inflation *is* rising prices, like the proponents of the Consumer Price Index claim, then inflation only occurs at the moment a price rises. Under this belief, it is the business owners who are responsible for inflation since they are the ones who set the prices of their products. There is no causation for inflation before a businessperson decides to raise prices.

Following this train of thought, if the source of rising prices is the "greedy businesspeople", then the solution is price controls, which are when the government makes it illegal to charge above or below a certain amount. If price ceilings are enforced - meaning prices cannot be charged above a certain amount - but the money supply continues to increase, the result is shortages, because people have increasing amounts of money with which to buy products, but the prices are kept down by the force of government.

The kind of money that we use dramatically impacts the relationship between the people and the government. If we were on a 100% commodity-backed money system, the only way that the government could get more money would be to take it from the people, or maybe to open up some mines, which would still be financed through taxes. The government, therefore is dependent on the people. This would make it very clear that new spending proposals meant higher taxes. Great increases in spending would be much harder to get approved by the public. However, when the government has the power to create money, it is no longer dependent on the people, and can fund its programs without always needing to resort to taxes. This can foster the misperception that rather than the government being dependent on the public, it is supporting them.

Think about how large a government can get when it has to tax people directly for the money it wants to spend versus when it can create the money it wants. The difference is that a government dealing in commodity-backed money will be much smaller than a government using fiat currency.

* * *

Imagine a small town where each person has $100 in their vault and in the middle of the night the Fair Inflation Angel comes to make everyone twice as rich. Everyone wakes up the next morning to find $200 in their vault. But each also has the knowledge that everyone else has doubled their money as well. What would happen? Well, the business owners would raise their prices twice as much, labor would cost twice as much, etc. There would be no change at all. Each dollar that they had before would now be worth half of its previous value. Obviously there is no point in this kind of inflation because there are zero benefits. Why then is there inflation?

Let's construct a scenario more like the real world, where there are limited benefits to inflation. Rather than being equally distributed throughout the economy all at once with everyone having perfect knowledge of what happened, let us imagine that the Federal Reserve prints up $1 million and loans it to the government. The government now spends the money in exchange for products and services. They are able to buy a lot with their money because the purchasing power of the dollar has not changed yet. Businesses which provided those products and services now also have nearly new money. They raise their prices, and spend their new money before others raise theirs. In this way the new money slowly works its way through the economy, effecting people in very uneven ways. Those who get the money first get a huge benefit, while those left out end up paying higher prices for goods while they still take home the same amount, such as those on a fixed income. This makes it clear that inflation is not necessary, but that it is done by choice to benefit those who get the new money early on and to harm those who get the money late or not at all.

> Inflation is a method of taxation which the government uses to secure the command over real resources; resources just as real as those obtained by ordinary taxation. What is raised by printing notes is just as much taken from the public as is an income tax. A government can live by this means when it can live by no other. It is the form of taxation that the public finds hardest to evade, and even the weakest government can enforce it when it can enforce no other.
>
> John Maynard Keynes,
> *The Economic Consequences of Peace*, 1920

The government's ability to inflate is a bit like magic for many people. The government is able to create an extensive array of welfare programs without having to directly tax people very much, thus giving the impression that it is providing these social services for free. While the benefits of the programs are touted all day long, the costs are rarely mentioned. Many wonder how others can possibly be opponents of free programs. When the costs are not realized by the public, there are calls for more programs, and thus the government grows.

CONSEQUENCES OF INFLATION

Inflation acts to *decrease savings* because people's incentive to save is decreased when they know that a dollar saved today will only be worth a fraction of that in a few years or further down the road when retirement comes. For those on low or fixed-incomes, more of their money needs to be spent buying the same goods because prices are rising, thus leaving less money with which to save. These are key factors in explaining the present low personal savings rate.

Inflation leads to *over-consumption* because people think they are wealthier than they are and therefore buy things they cannot really afford.

Inflation has undesirable consequences on *profit* and *taxes*, from the tax-payers perspective. Inflation makes businesses think they are more profitable than they are, putting them in higher tax brackets and making it harder and harder to replace capital goods. This radically undercuts the ability of a business to stay in business, let alone expand. This is in contrast to the public perception that inflation is caused by corporate greed. The consequences are the same when we are dealing with personal income. As inflation continues, the nominal amount we make increases, which pushes us into higher tax brackets, even though the purchasing power of the money has actually decreased. People often end up thinking they are wealthier than they actually are and not saving appropriately.

Think about how people in general view purchasing a house as an investment for the future. Even in the current down housing market, the people who are buying are assuming the prices will go back up later. This is a form of wasteful investment because the only way that general house prices can increase is due to inflation. Of course, if all houses started off the same price, certain properties would get bid up due to increased demand, such as New York City and San Francisco. But while those places are being bid up, other places would be dropping in price, so that the general price level would stay the same.

To illustrate how inflation effects the housing market, let's first look at the housing market without inflation. Houses would act like any other product, where over time, through technological advances, their quality increases and their price stays the same or decreases. If you bought a house now, and knew that you could buy a better one in 10 years for the same or less money, you would not consider it an investment but rather a consumption good - that is something you get use out of but does not pay for its own replacement. In 10 years then, how much would your 10 year old house be worth? It certainly would not be worth as much as the new and better ones. As with other products which are not collector's items, their value goes down over time.

However, if the money supply grows at about 8% per year, then housing prices will go up by approximately the same amount. When people expect that home prices will continue to rise, without being aware that the purchasing power of the dollar is going down, they are more likely to purchase a home. This gives them the benefit of living in the home while also making money off of it. This leads many more homes to be constructed than would be otherwise, thereby diverting many resources from other industries to housing.

If the rate of inflation were high enough, people might start "investing" in automobiles or even bicycles because a couple of years after they were purchased, their nominal values would be higher than when they were originally bought.

> Lenin is said to have declared that the best way to destroy the capitalist system was to debauch the currency. By a continuing process of inflation, governments can confiscate secretly and unobserved, an important part of the wealth of their citizens...Lenin was certainly right. The process engages all the hidden forces of economic law on

the side of destruction, and does so in a manner which only one man in a million is able to diagnose.

John Maynard Keynes,
British economist, 1920

Eliminating inflation would *increase* capital accumulation, which is the foundation of a rising productivity of labor which leads to a higher standard of living. Since inflation only occurs due to the force of government, violating people's property rights, its elimination would also be the moral approach.

CASE STUDY: *Hyperinflation*

After World War I, Germany was in a bad state and had to come up with the 132 billion gold marks it owed for reparations. It turned to the printing press and started rolling out paper money. In January of 1919, it took 12 German Marks to buy an ounce of silver. At this time a Mark was roughly equivalent to an American Dollar. By November 30, 1923 it took 543,750,000,000 German Marks to purchase an ounce of silver. Whereas a person could retire comfortably in 1919 with 50,000 Marks in the bank, by 1923 bank accounts with 50,000 Marks were being closed due to insufficient funds, and the postage on an envelope cost 2,000,000 Marks.

Hyperinflation is one of the worst preventable things that can happen to an economy. With no monetary stability, savings goes down to nothing as people have to spend money as soon as they get it because it is rapidly losing value. This will very quickly lead an economy to ruin because without savings there is no capital investment. This should remind us that wealth is not measured by how high the number on the bill is, but rather the goods and services for which it can be exchanged. In Germany, there were trillionaires and quadrillionaires, but that does not mean they were living the life of luxury.

Do Lower Prices Mean Deflation and Depression?

Recessions and depressions do not occur with precious metal money, they occur with fractional-reserve banking. The key reason is that once gold or silver come into existence, by way of digging them out of the ground, they do not go out of existence. Money that is created out of thin air can disappear into thin air as well, and this is what causes a decrease in the quantity of money.

In a commodity-money economy, total spending would almost never decrease because the supply of money would not sharply decrease, making it both deflation and inflation proof.

Since people usually think of inflation as rising prices, many often think of falling prices as deflation. There have been numerous times when this has been the case, all of which were caused by the fractional-reserve banking system. When the supply of money decreases, the supply of goods and their prices tend to fall (if they are allowed to). On the other hand, if we are experiencing increases in production which outstrip the increases in the money supply, what is the result? Lower prices. However, this situation of lower prices is radically different from deflation. In this case, increased production is leading to an increased supply of goods, and even though the average price and wage will fall, the purchasing power of the money has gone up so that people are actually able to buy more with less.

Those who believe that it is generally lowering prices which cause depression are actually believing that it is too much prosperity which causes poverty. In an economy with a stable supply of money, the way that prices would go down would be through increases in production. These increases in production allow people of all different means to have access to goods, thereby raising the general level of prosperity. Thinking that this lowering of prices is what causes depressions and poverty is completely backwards. Lower general prices in an economy with a stable money supply is a sign of more people being able to meet their needs and desires. The key is to see one's wealth not as the nominal amount of one's bank account, but how much you can buy with that money. We are not impoverished by the process of growing richer.

The only similarity between depression and an increase in production greater than the increase in the money supply is falling prices. Whereas in a depression debtors have a harder time paying back their debts, when prices are falling due to increased production, debtors have an easier time paying the money back because there are more sales. Also, the money that the creditors get back is actually more valuable than the money originally lent, in that the purchasing power has increased. Thus production which increases faster than the money supply is of benefit to both creditors and debtors.

LEGAL TENDER

While I am not a proponent of fiat currency and inflation, I see them as relatively harmless without legal tender laws, which the state uses to force people to use its currency. If people in a free market have a choice between gold and a piece of paper with no backing, with education most people will likely choose the precious metal currency. The silver currency created by Liberty Dollar was able to become as widespread as it was because the recipients of the silver readily saw the value. However, if there are laws which say that taxes must be paid with the fiat currency, and the paper money must be accepted in payment of private debts as well, then people will greatly diminish their use of the commodity money. Making people accept something that they see as worthless pieces of paper is an act of force. People will tend to adopt as the general money whatever is required to pay taxes. Coercion is never necessary to get people to use something they already see value in, such as commodity-money.

Dimes were made of 90% silver until 1946 when they were changed to a combination of copper and nickel. Both dimes had the same face value and could circulate freely, but since silver had a higher value on the market, people began to hoard those dimes and spend the new ones. There is actually a principle in economics to describe this called Gresham's Law, which states that money artificially overvalued by government will drive out artificially undervalued money from circulation.

CENTRAL BANKING

Despite what you may have heard in the mainstream media or economics courses about central banks being created to stabilize economies, just the opposite is true. A central bank is a bank with a government granted monopoly on the issuance of the notes people must use to pay taxes. Since private banks are prohibited from issuing these notes, they all must become members of the Central Bank. In this way the Central Bank is considered a "banker's bank" and is the lender of last resort. They also hold the power of determining the interest rates on loaned money. Central banks are established to plunder the wealth of the people through inflation and boom and bust cycles.

Counterfeiting has a bad reputation, as it should. But we need to look at who is really doing the counterfeiting here. Central banks are institutions which have a legal monopoly to counterfeit money. You can't just copy gold, silver, shells, etc., but Federal Reserve Notes are money created out of nothing, and then copied billions of times with minimal effort. This is wonderful for the previously private banks. Now they do not have to worry about reserves or bank runs, because they can always get more money from the central bank.

> I believe that banking institutions are more dangerous to our liberties than standing armies.
>
> Thomas Jefferson,
> U.S. President, 1787

Central banks have been around since 1694, when Scottish financier William Patterson and the King William III of England joined forces to create the Bank of England. With the consent of the government, the Bank of England fraudulently multiplied their warehouse receipts so that there were more paper claims to gold than actual gold. They would then loan out the fake receipts as real money and charge interest on them. This was the first time that fractional-reserve banking was institutionalized. The central bank works by creating all of the money that is used by the government. All new money is created by being loaned into existence, whether to the government, businesses, or private individuals.

THE FEDERAL RESERVE

> Centralization of credit in the hands of the State, by means of a national bank with State capital and an exclusive monopoly.
>
> 5th Plank of communism,
> *The Communist Manifesto*,
> Karl Marx & Friedrich Engels, 1848

Take a dollar out of your wallet and look it over. You will notice at the top it says Federal Reserve Note. I never paid much attention to it. A dollar was a dollar in my mind. How wrong I was! The

Federal Reserve is the central bank for the United States. It is a privately owned joint-stock trust, created by the world's wealthiest bankers in 1913. The Federal Reserve is only quasi-governmental. The banks themselves are privately owned, but the reason we have to use their currency is because of the Federal Reserve Act and the Legal Tender laws. The Federal Reserve Act authorized the Federal Reserve banking system to extend to the United States as much credit as is needed to expand its operations. It is the force of government which compels people to partake in this monetary system.

It is my contention that the detrimental effect the Federal Reserve is having on our economy is due not to the degree to which it is private, as some believe, but rather to *how connected it is to the government*. This connection is what allows the Fed to force people to use its currency. Without force, the Federal Reserve would wither away.

The prosperity level of Americans was improving during much of the 1800's without a central bank, and they were hard to convince that they needed one. Artificially created bank panics (e.g., 1857, 1873, 1893, 1907) created the appearance of a problem that was used to discredit the decentralized banking system, and used as justification for the creation of the Federal Reserve System in 1913.

While its stated goals are to stabilize the economy, its track record speaks for itself: the crashes of 1921 and 1929, the Great Depression, recessions of 1953, '57, '69, '75 and '81, the stock market "Black Monday" of 1987, the current depression (which may turn out to be the most ruinous in history), and the loss of 98% of the dollar's value over the last 98 years.

Since its inception, the Federal Reserve has been creating money out of nothing. How does this work? All of the money that constitutes our money supply was authorized by the Federal Reserve, whether they are bills or just numbers on a ledger. Not all of it was created by the Fed, as much of what is in circulation was created by "private" banks. All of our money is debt-based because it was all loaned into existence.

> A Federal Reserve Note is merely an IOU. Here's how it works. When the politicians want more money, they dispatch a request to the Federal Reserve for whatever sum they desire. The Bureau of Printing and Engraving then prints up bonds indenturing taxpayers to redeem their debts. The bonds are then 'sold' to the Federal Reserve. But note this unusual twist. the bonds are paid for with a check backed by nothing! It is as if you were to look into your account and see a balance of $505 and then, hearing government bonds were for sale, write a draft for $1 billion. Of course, if you did that you would go to jail. The bankers do not. In effect, they print the money that enables their check to clear.
>
> James Davidson, Director,
> National Taxpayers Union

As we have advised, the Federal Reserve is currently paying the Bureau approximately $23 for each 1,000 notes printed. This does include the cost of printing, paper, ink, labor, etc. Therefore, 10,000 notes of any denomination, including the $100 note would cost the Federal Reserve $230. In addition, the Federal Reserve must secure a pledge of collateral equal to the face value of the notes.

William H. Ferkler, Manager Public Affairs, Dept.
of Treasury, Bureau of Engraving and Printing, 1994

The Federal Reserve acts against the public interest by engineering major bailouts of corporations which have failed. This benefits only the stockholders of those companies, and puts the rest of us further in debt. The Federal Reserve also encourages war because without its fiat currency, most wars would either not be possible or would be greatly reduced in scale. But if a government can just create new money for a war, then many more and larger wars are possible.

> Those who create and issue credit and money, direct the policies of government, and hold in the hollow of their hands the destiny of the people.
> Reginald McKenna, former Chancellor of the Exchequer, England

> Whoever controls the money in any country is master of all its legislation and commerce.
> James Garfield,
> U.S. President, 1831-1881

THE NATIONAL DEBT

While many people believe that we have trillions of dollars of debt because we live beyond our means, this overlooks the fundamental reason. Sure, if the government didn't spend so much, and people and businesses didn't take out so many loans, we wouldn't have as much debt - but there would still be a lot, and it would still be inescapable.

Why?

Because of where the money comes from. It is all debt-based, meaning that the money is borrowed into existence. As you can see, if money is created out of nothing, and then loaned with interest to the people who legally have to use it under Legal Tender laws, then the people can never pay off the debt. It is mathematically impossible because there is always more debt to pay than there is money to pay it with. If all of the loans were paid off there would not be a cent in circulation, and there would still be loads of debt. Currently, the more money there is in circulation, the greater our debt load.

> If all the bank loans were paid no one would have a bank deposit and there would be not a dollar or coin or currency in circulation. This is a staggering thought. We are completely dependent on the commercial banks. Someone has to borrow every dollar into circulation. If the banks create ample synthetic money, we are prosperous; if not, we starve. We are absolutely without a permanent money system. When one gets a complete grasp of the picture, the tragic absurdity of our hopeless position is almost incredible, but there it is. It is the most important subject intelligent persons can investigate and reflect upon. It is so important that our present civilization may collapse unless it becomes widely understood and the defects remedied very soon.
>
> Robert Hemphill, former Credit Manager,
> Federal Reserve Bank of Atlanta,
> in testimony before the Senate, 1935

So when the politicians talk about budget deficit and budget surplus, that is just a matter of how much they tax us versus how much they spend. If they have a surplus, then they taxed us more than they spent. But none of this deals with the national debt, which they do not want to talk about.

The only way for there not to be a national debt is to not have the money loaned into existence in the first place, and for there to be no monopoly control - whether by a government or central bank - over the creation of money and the manipulation of interest rates. A large portion of our taxes go to paying just the interest on this debt, which is completely unnecessary. Our productivity and our property are being taxed to pay for the existence of our money. Does that sound crazy or what?

As we learned earlier in this chapter, money does not need to be loaned into existence because it arises naturally. We can simply choose to have a free market in money and use the currency which best meets our needs.

ALL BANK LOANS ARE VOID

This was one of the more startling truths I came across in my research into banking. If our economy were just 10 people, then we would easily see the fraudulent nature of fractional-reserve banking, but the fact that we have hundreds of millions involved in the U.S. economy, and billions globally makes it much less obvious to one's senses.

Banks put up no real money for the loans. They create the money out of nothing and charge interest on it. When making a loan the note has to be supported by lawful consideration (the thing of value which is exchanged).

Mortgages, as well as other types of bank loans, are collectively impossible to make good on. Under State Civil Codes, as well as basic ethics, a contract which is impossible to perform is inherently void. Why are bank loans impossible contracts? Every loan that is created merely brings the principal money into existence but not the interest money that is required as payment on top of the principal. In a large economy it is difficult to see that everyone is paying the interest on their debts with the principal from other people's loans. The only way that this system can carry on is by continually making new loans. However, even if the quantity of money is increased, it is still mathematically impossible to pay off all of the loans.

Here are the very simple equations which show that not all people can pay off their bank loans:

P = Principal; I = Total Interest Payment.
P/(P+I) = Percentage loaned money that *will be able to be paid off*
I/(P+I) = Percentage of loaned money *will be defaulted on*

For example, let's say there are a $1 billion in principal loans. Let's say the total interest payments on this amount is $60 million. $1 billion/$1.06 billion = 94.34% of loaned money will be able to be paid off. $60 million/$1.06 billion = 5.66% of loaned money will be defaulted on.

In a system in which money comes into existence only by borrowing at interest, the system as a whole is always short on funds, and somebody has to default. It may seem contradictory that fractional-reserve banking can lead to both too much money in the economy (inflation) and too little (unavoidable defaults) at the same time. Unfortunately, these are both true statements and that is exactly why our economic system is not sustainable. We have gone over the deleterious effects of inflation, but in our fractional-reserve money system, if the supply of money is not perpetually increased, a massive amount of people and businesses will be forced to default, resulting in a depression.

First National Bank of Montgomery vs. Daly was a 1964 court case which blew open, however briefly, the veil of the banking institution. Mr. Daly, who was an attorney, defended himself against the bank's attempt to foreclose his $14,000 property, saying that they did not put up any lawful consideration in support of the loan. While people were skeptical of Daly's defense at first, once Mr. Morgan, the bank's president, took the stand, the opinions of Presiding Justice Martin Mahoney and the jurors radically shifted to supporting Mr. Daly and condemning Mr. Morgan. Justice Mahoney recorded his thoughts afterward:

> Plaintiff admitted that it, in combination with the Federal Reserve Bank of Minneapolis, ... did create the entire $14,000 in money and credit upon its own books by bookkeeping entry. That this was the consideration used to support the Note dated May, 8 1964 and the mortgage of the same date. The money and credit first came into existence when they created it. Mr. Morgan admitted that no United States Law or Statute existed which gave him the right to do this. A lawful consideration must exist and be tendered to support the Note.

The Justice declared the banks actions fraudulent and allowed Mr. Daly to keep his home. While the implications of this should have dramatically changed banking for the better, that did not happen because judges since then have not been as courageous as Justice Mahoney, in that they are unwilling to side against a bank for fear of being the one to shake the status quo.

THE INTERNATIONAL MONETARY FUND AND THE WORLD BANK

In 1944, the International Monetary Fund and the World Bank were created with the proclaimed goals of facilitating international trade and stabilizing exchange rates. That sounds great, however their true goals were the elimination of the international gold-exchange standard and the promotion of socialism. How did they do this? Rather than dealing with gold, which is harder to control, the IMF, acting as the central bank for the world, would make money out of nothing and then the World Bank would transfer the money to the governments of underdeveloped countries. This influx of money has the twin effects of expanding the governments and crippling the economies because the people are working to pay off these big loans that were made out of thin air. They are kept in poverty and often lose their land, resources and businesses as collateral.

The Socialist International, a worldwide organization of socialists, has stated that the IMF is "in essence a Socialist conception." At the inception of the IMF, the free market economist Henry Hazlitt was one of the few who understood what it was and tried to expose it. He wrote that "the world cannot get back to economic sanctity until the IMF is abolished... We will not stop the growth of world inflation and world socialism until the institutions and policies adopted to promote them have been abolished." (Jasper, 2001)

THE BUSINESS CYCLE IS NOT NATURAL

For nearly a hundred years now the reasons why the economy goes through cycles of booms and busts, often referred to as "business cycles", have been known, though unfortunately not widely so.

The so-called business cycle is the artificial expansion of the economy followed necessarily by its contraction. This is a very important concept to understand at this time because we are in a depression, and if you immerse yourself in the media you may just get the wrong idea of what causes this to occur.

Of course, if everyone paid all of their bills, and the banks only loaned out wisely, things would be better. But we need to look deeper, because while the industry that booms and busts may change over time, the cycle itself does not. The same expansion and contraction has been going on for as long as there has been fractional-reserve banking.

It was Ludwig von Mises who pierced the veil in the early 1900's and saw the controlled, inner workings of the business cycle. And this cycle will continue on and on, ravaging our economy, unless we wise up and take control of our money and our lives.

It is a very simplistic view that many economists and lay people hold about the business cycle and what needs to be done. If there is rapid inflation, that means there is too much private spending, and to curb this, taxes are increased. If there is a recession, that means there is too little spending, and the government spreads the message that it will solve this problem by increasing its own expenditures. Free markets, they believe, are the cause of the ups and downs, and government is there to correct the economy and keep it on track.

So if the free market is not to blame, then who is, and how do these business cycles come about?

The two important concepts that you learned earlier in this chapter that underlie the business cycle are *fiat currency* and *inflation*. These economic booms and busts simply could not occur if the money was commodity-based, and there was no inflation, meaning banks would have a one-hundred percent reserve ratio. In a free market, supply and demand tend toward equilibrium. But when the government sets an interest rate that is lower than the free market rate, the commercial banks expand credit, and businesses take advantage of this cheap money by taking out loans, thereby increasing the money supply. This cheaper money stimulates the economy by making certain business ventures appear profitable, which under the free market interest rate seemed unprofitable.

All of these new business enterprises act to increase the demand for production materials and labor. This increased demand leads to higher prices for the factors of production, including wages, which result in higher prices for consumer goods. As more money is pumped into the economy, prices rise even more. When the labor and other productive means are used in these new ventures, they are diverted from one's which were profitable before money became cheaper. For a while, so long as new money is created, people will not notice this diversion. While increasing the money supply is a good way to get an economy into trouble, further increases will not right the ship. Once the process of inflation starts there are two bad possible endings, though one far worse than the other.

The worse way is to continue the process of inflation which leads to prices rising faster and faster. Once people become aware that there is no foreseeable end to the quickly rising prices, they start to panic. No one wants to hold onto money which is rapidly becoming worthless, so people move to exchange the money for goods as fast as they can, even if the good is not something they normally would have purchased. Ultimately, when the value of the money drops to almost nothing, the currency collapses, bringing the economy down with it, such as happened in Germany in 1923.

The choice which is not as bad as hyperinflation is if the banks severely tighten credit before the collapse of the monetary system.

This restriction will immediately bring to light the wasteful investments which the entrepreneurs had thought were profitable due to inflation, as many businesses have to cut back operations or close altogether. The artificial expansion of part of the economy due to easy credit and low interest rates results in economic contraction as businesses fail, and much of the capital that was invested is locked up in unprofitable buildings and factories. Any further lowering of the interest rate once the depression has set in will only stimulate the economy in the very short run, and will lead to a prolonging of the economic contraction.

When the supply of money is contracted by increased interest rates the economy suffers as the goods people worked to acquire are taken as collateral for defaulted loans. So as the credit is increased people consume more, and when credit then becomes tight those goods go to the banks.

If we see a big bubble building or we are already in a slowing economy, as we are now, then what are we to do? The Fed needs to relinquish control of the interest rate. It will then go to its market determined level, which will be much higher than it currently is, and people will suffer in the short run as the economy corrects itself. Unfortunately this is not the course of action the Fed ever takes. The economy needs to correct itself by lowering prices and wages and reallocating resources to where people most value them. If the free market is allowed to determine the interest rate, the correction period will be relatively short, while if the Fed continues to lower the rate in order to increase spending, the correction will be prolonged.

In this time when higher interest rates would actually be good, they continue to lower the rate to "stimulate" the economy. As we have just gone over, this is false stimulation and will only prolong the economic woes. But since many people do not realize this, every time the Fed comes out and says it will boost the economy by lowering the interest rate, people cheer and the stock markets surge upwards.

Every time the economy slows it is blamed on the free market and lack of regulation. As Alan Greenspan stated in October of 2008, "I had too much faith in the free market." So what is the response that politicians and many in the public call for? Greater regulation. And that is exactly what has been happening. Control over more and more of the markets is put in the hands of bureaucrats - the same bureaucrats who caused the economic downturn in the first place with their policies.

CASE STUDY: *Lessons from the Great Depression*

We are now in one of the worst depressions since the Great Depression, and while it may seem as if it was a whole different world back then, the similarities are striking, and it is important for us to understand what caused the Great Depression and what made it last for so long. If we are not able to grasp this basic understanding, and the same actions are taken which during the 1930's prolonged the Depression, then we will experience the same dreadful results, or worse.

Following a sharp recession during 1920-21, which was a result of massive inflation during World War I, the Roaring Twenties shot out of the gate by way of the expansionary monetary policy of the Federal Reserve and foreign central banks. This boom lasted from mid-1921 until mid-1929, during which the supply of money increased from $45.3 billion to $73.3 billion, a 61.8% increase. However, the physical currency in circulation did not expand, staying at around $3.66 billion. All of the monetary expansion, therefore, took place in money-substitutes, as government regulations encouraged margin investing, which means that people were trading with money they either did not own or could not easily produce.

From October 24th, 1929 until July 8, 1932, the *New York Times* industrials had fallen from 452 points down to 58, a drop of more than 87%. Industrial production fell by more than half between 1929 and 1933, manufactured durables fell by 77%, and business construction plummeted from $8.7 billion down to $1.4 billion. The money supply fell by more than 25%, and credit was unobtainable by all but the strongest of businesses, leading to many bankruptcies and a dramatic increase in financial conservatism for many years.

During this time, unemployment rose from a modest 3.2% to a high of 26.7% in 1934. As union power increased in the early thirties, they actually drove wages up, even while there was mass unemployment, which lasted until the United States entered World War II. As economies of the world were and are connected, the depression spread to other parts of the globe, and some countries, such as France, were not able to get back to their 1929 level of production until the mid-1950's.

Even though there was full employment during World War II, it did not lead to prosperity because it was the result of inflation, price and wage freezes, rationing and a reduced workforce. The prosperity came back to America post-war, when there was the largest government spending reduction in its history, from $100 billion in 1944 to $38 billion in 1946. This capital and the 8 million discharged soldiers flowed into the private sector and worked to produce goods that people wanted. (Reisman, 1997)

Many people consider the Great Depression the final dagger in the heart of capitalism. It is often believed that it was the unrestrained market which led to the stock market crash, and that the government had to battle the forces of the free market for the next decade until it finally won, allowing people to again start to raise their standard of living. Nothing could be further from the truth.

The boom during the 1920's was only possible because government regulation encouraged fractional-reserve banking, which is inherently fraudulent. And then the government would not allow the market to correct itself as it continued to pump in inflationary credit. The economic tragedy of the Depression Era was not a result of the unrestrained market, but rather a clear example of the problems of government intervention.

The administrations of Presidents Hoover and Roosevelt were almost completely in alignment in their approach to conquer the faltering economy. Roosevelt is looked upon more favorably in the history books merely because he was better at public relations. Their plans were the same, but Roosevelt expanded them, taking far more of the tax-payer's money.

The inflationary policy of the Federal Reserve which allowed for the bubble to form during the 1920's, continued when the stock market crashed. During the last *week* of October, 1929, the money supply was increased by %10, and interest rates were decreased.

President Hoover was already prepared with an interventionist approach to solve the economic collapse. He argued for all states to increase their public works programs, which are tax-payer supported jobs. He implemented the New Deal farm program which primarily focused on price supports. It was Hoover's decisive action in late 1929 that led many to believe that a crisis had been averted and better times were around the corner. While an unemployment rate of 9% was high at this time, it was nowhere close to as bad as it was going to get.

Against the recommendations of many of the day's economists, President Hoover signed into law the Smoot-Hawley tariff. He mistakenly believed that high tariffs help farmers by building up domestic demand and decreasing dependence on export markets, therefore bolstering the U.S. economy. Upon signing this bill, the stock market took another tumble which spread throughout the world as countries realized that protectionism was now the name of the game. This led to hobbled international division of labor, which decreased worldwide production and trade.

Hoover countered declines in production, prices, foreign trade and employment by attacking the property rights of creditors, in the form of weakening bankruptcy laws and banning immigration, unless you were particularly wealthy. This attempt to reduce unemployment by reducing the labor force was similar to Hitler's later move of forcing married women back in the home - none of which are necessary if wages are allowed to be set by the market.

Hoover's approach to curing the depression consisted of using the Federal Reserve to supposedly promote stability by increasing credit at low rates, as well as tax-funded programs and public works projects. He was also able to get an agreement from employers not to lower their wage rates, even while prices were falling. Now that you are familiar with the difference between nominal wages and purchasing power, you can see that the effect of holding wages steady while the price of goods goes down is to actually *increase* the employees' real wages (purchasing power). Even when wage rates finally did start to fall after the first two years of the depression wiped out profits, they did not fall as fast as the prices, so those employed still had real wages which were increasing. During 1930 and 1931, average wage rates dropped less than 2.5% and about 6.5%, respectively. During the short-lived depression of 1920-21, wage rates fell 19% in a single year

(Reisman, 1997). This equalization of prices and wages helped the recovery to be swift.

In 1931, while the gross national product and gross private product fell severely over the previous year, government spending substantially increased. Remember that governments can only spend by taking from the people, whether by taxes or by inflation. So along with the prescribed inflation, Hoover also decided to drastically increase personal income taxes, estate taxes, sales taxes and postal rates. The Revenue Act of 1932 marked one of the largest increases in people's tax-load during a time of peace in American history. Sales taxes were imposed on gasoline, tires, autos, electricity, malt, toiletries, furs, jewelry, and many wartime excise taxes were reintroduced. New taxes were placed upon telephone, telegraph and radio messages, and the gift tax was restored at up to 33.3%.

In 1933, both federal and state governments began to seriously undermine people's property rights as they related to their money. Many states decided to have compulsory debt moratoria - a temporary suspension of debt and interest payments. Between 1932 and 1933, the number of bank failures shot up from 1,453 to 4,000. One major problem with the fractional-reserve system is that it really is like a giant game of musical chairs, where there actually is not enough money to go around. What this means is that each dollar has multiple claims of ownership on it, so when there is a run on the bank, there simply is not enough money for each person to get what is supposedly safe in their account.

When people saw some banks failing, their confidence in the banks shattered and they went to withdraw their cash. State by state instituted "bank holidays", which meant that people were not allowed to get their money out of the bank, but the bank was allowed to stay in business. It is at these times when it becomes very clear the destructive and fraudulent nature of fractional-reserve banking. *Fractional-reserve banking* and *respect for property rights are absolutely incompatible.* Between March 6th and March 13th of 1933, President Roosevelt declared a national "bank holiday", in which the banks of the nation were closed for the entire week, and some for longer.

With the national banking system was in crisis, Roosevelt chose the path of more government controls. The "bank holidays" stripped depositors of their property rights, people's gold was confiscated under threat of posting a public list of who owned how much gold, and the government ended up with greater control of the nation's economy. Since the government put an end to the American gold standard in 1933, almost every year since has been an inflationary one.

So what would happen if instead of increased government regulations there was a free market approach? Once there is an inflationary boom, it has to correct, and that will not be pretty no matter what. The question is, will it be quick, or will it be long and agonizing, in such a way that will lead to more booms and busts in the future? The quickest, smoothest way for an economy to get out of a recession or depression is to have no government intervention, whether it is in business, banking, money supply, interest rates, price and wage controls, bankruptcy, subsidies, tax hikes, etc. Allowing prices and wage rates to adjust according to the market would mean that after the market corrected, there could be full employment. This is because wage regulations, among other regulations, are primarily responsible for unemployment in the first place. When wage rates fall to their equilibrium, investment spending increases, which restores general business profitability.

Not bailing out failing companies (with tax-payer money) would mean that those businesses which are unsound would go bankrupt, while those which are sound would survive. When a business believes that it will be rescued, it is much more likely to take big risks. The banks would be allowed to fail as well, with the depositors taking over control of what was left. A massive deflation would ensue which would bring the paper money supply down to nearly completely backed by gold (and/or silver). This would quickly end the fraudulent practice of fractional-reserve banking. And we would have been on our way probably within less than a year toward the most sound money system the world had ever seen, which would have been the backbone of a level of prosperity the world had never seen, far beyond where we are today.

You may be wondering what would be happening to people's lives while these companies are failing. When there is an economic contraction, we have to face the fact that there are going to be some hard times. However, those hard times will be much less painful if free market solutions are not prevented from occurring. There will be short-term unemployment as some businesses shrink or collapse altogether, but in the longer term those employees will move to areas in the market which are stronger and where their services are more valued.

Unfortunately, we are now headed down the same path that led to a protracted depression in the 1930's. We need to learn the lessons and take appropriate action, or inaction in some cases. During 2008 and 2009, there were some high profile bailouts totaling $8.5 *trillion*, including $400 billion to Fannie Mae and Freddie Mac and the $700 billion Wall Street Band-Aid.

Even though it was the government which caused the Great Depression, it blamed it on the free market, and claimed the need for more government control over the economy, which it got. Since then, we have seen boom and bust after boom and bust, and now the government, which once again is completely responsible for the depression, is blaming it on a lack of regulation. They are now wanting, and getting, even more control over our money and our lives. We really cannot keep giving the perpetrators more power and expecting different results, namely the mirage of a government-stabilized economy.

TOWARD A WORLD CURRENCY AND FINANCIAL SYSTEM

With those in government blaming the global economic downturn on lack of regulation, their solution is for more centralized control of the world economic systems. In the U.S., the government has already started to take ownership of some banks and buy shares in many more. There are talks from governments around the world for tighter regulation, and the need for a central bank for the world along with a global currency. It shouldn't surprise us that the people who caused the problem and have the power, seek greater power while placing the responsibility on others.

While a single currency for the world may be down the road a bit, the next step will likely be more regional currencies, like the Euro. So what would the world be like with a single currency? Well, there are some important distinctions to make. I am not at all opposed to having one currency for the world. The fewer currencies there are, the easier trade becomes. People do not have to worry about exchange rates, and they can spend their money anywhere in the world. However, my vision for a world currency would be one which is 100% commodity-based, that arose naturally on the free market, and became the currency of choice voluntarily rather than by force. People would be free to stop using the predominant currency and start using their own or a competing currency. This sort of worldwide monetary system would have tremendous benefits for trade while eliminating the booms and busts of the business cycle.

As you can probably guess, this is not anything close to what the government officials are calling for when they are demanding a global currency. What they want is a fiat currency like the Euro, maybe called the Globo, with fractional-reserve banking. Right now, if one or several currencies are devaluing quickly, people can purchase other currencies to hedge against inflation. But if there is only one type of money that people are forced to use, and it is inherently inflationary, then people have nowhere to go. A global central bank and monetary system are simply ways of getting more control over people's lives. While the push for the currency may come under the rubric of worldwide economic stability, the results will be anything but. The American economy has not enjoyed the stability that the creation of the Federal Reserve was supposed to bring. A central financial system for the world will yield similar, and likely worse results. That is why we need to learn from our past, and not be sucked in by the siren-song of government omniscience.

WHAT IS THE SOLUTION?

If our money was commodity-based (e.g. silver and/or gold), and our banking system used 100% reserve, then all of these manipulated booms and busts would cease to occur. I want you to read that sentence again and feel the power. A sound monetary system would be one based on weight, where prices are indicated in a unit of weight such as grams or ounces. While different languages would have different words for the unit of measurement, they would be referring to the same thing. In this system, without looking you could tell the difference between $5 and $100 worth of gold when placed in your hand. Compare this with fiat currency where a piece of paper can have a 1, 10, 100 or a much higher number printed on it. If your eyes were closed you would not be able to tell if you were holding more or less money in your hand.

Wealth is not just about numbers on a piece of paper but about goods, and the more goods there are the wealthier we are. Our monetary system should not be separated from this basic truth.

> Persons who don't know the differences between gold and paper don't know the difference between reality and dreams, so let them pay for living in the *ideasphere* by giving up their property to the tentacles of inflation.
>
> F. Tupper Saussy,
> *The Miracle on Main St.,* 1980

What we need is not more regulation. What we need is to use real money, and have its value derived by the free market not controlled centrally by an elite group. Under this system, prices would likely fall since productivity would probably increase faster than new metals would be found and made useable. This would also have the very significant advantage of preventing deflation depression as well as inflation.

In order for us to prosper in the long run, our money system must not be centrally controlled. Let's look past the political rhetoric, and see the current system for what it is: a way to control people's lives. Isn't it interesting that by just manipulating a number (the interest rate), people's lives can completely change? That is why they want control of it. If the free market decided the interest rates, it would not go up or down based on the whims of a small group. It would change based on supply and demand - a fundamental principle of economics.

Prior to 1933, when Roosevelt confiscated people's gold and divorced the dollar from it, the dollar was defined as 23.22 grains of gold. Since there are 480 grains in a troy ounce, an ounce of gold was valued at $20.67. Today the price of an ounce of gold is around $1600. Accordingly, a $100 bill today is worth about $1.29 of 1932 dollars. [100/(1600/20.67) = 1.29] If the real value of money was printed on the dollars, this would help to wake people up to how much purchasing power they have lost over time. Today's $200,000 homes would be $2,583 in 1932 dollars; $20,000 automobiles would be $258; the Dow Jones at 14,000 would be 180; the Dow Jones at 6,500 would be 84; $1,000 computers would be $12.90; $50/month phone bills would be $0.65/month; and today's $2.50 loaves of bread would cost about 3 cents.

Imagine that two elderly friends who were living in the U.S. 1914 and wanted to bury some treasure for their descendants. Each decided to hide $5,000. One chose the money to be in Federal Reserve Notes and the other chose for it to be in gold. They gave maps to their family and instructions to open it up in 2011. 97 years later, the two great-grandchildren search for the booty, digging in the ground for the buried treasure. When the first one reaches his box, he is excited to see the $5,000 still there, and still intact. The second one finds a heavy box filled with 263.3 ounces of gold [5000/18.99 = 263.3], worth about $421,274 [263.3 x 1600 = 421,274]. Which great-grandparent would you rather have? And which great-grandparent would you rather be for your descendants?

I Object!
Answers to Common Questions and Objections

In a 100% reserve system, how would the bankers make money?

It is true that the tallest buildings in each city most likely would not be banks if our money was completely backed by a commodity, but they would still be able to make the general rate of profit for business. Money which customers wanted access to as they pleased would be kept in a demand-deposit account. Banks would not be allowed to loan out this money, but they would be able to charge a storage fee. When money was to be transferred, they could charge a transfer fee as well. The other side of the business would be the loans, where the customers would place their money in a time-deposit with a guaranteed rate of return at the end of the given time period. The bank would be able to loan the actual money out, and get their interest payments on that, making money both for them and their customers. They would enjoy approximately the same rate of profit as the average business in the economy.

There wouldn't be enough gold to go around if it were used as money.

I agree that if only gold were used as money, the amounts that each person would have would be so small as to be nearly indivisible and would thus hinder trade. However, this does not rule out using gold as money. In a free market monetary system, gold would likely be used for more expensive purchases, and silver would probably be the common currency, which there is plenty of for everyone in the world to use in trade. The quantity of money does not need to increase in proportion to the rising levels of production, as some think. If the quantity of money stays the same or increases more slowly than the rise in production, the effect will be greater purchasing power. If the quantity of money is artificially increased to keep pace with production, we are still left with the problem of theft by inflation.

This can be tricky to understand, so let's use some examples.

Let's say that the total supply of money in the economy is $100, and there are 100 goods to purchase. The average price of each good then is $1.

If production has increased by 10% over the course of the year while the supply of money has stayed the same that would mean there was $100 to spend on 110 goods. Is each dollar worth more or less than it was the year before? It is worth more. The average price of each good is now $0.91 while before it was $1. This means that the purchasing power of the dollar has increased.

Now, let's look at this same situation, but rather than the money supply staying the same, it is artificially increased (just by printing more notes) to keep pace with production. Over the course of the year production increased the supply of goods to 110, and those in control of the money supply decide that it should increase as well to $110. So rather than the average price falling to $0.91 it stays at $1. What has happened to the purchasing power? It has stayed the same. If the money supply had stayed constant, the consumers would have been able to purchase approximately 9% more goods than if the money supply increases with production.

You can see how increasing the supply of money is not necessary but simply acts to take away wealth from the consumers.

On a commodity-based money system, the supply of money would likely increase, but rate of increase is the key. Over time, there would be maybe a 1 or 2% annual increase in the supply of the commodity being used as money. If the supply of money is increasing at 1 or 2% while the supply of goods is increasing at 4 or 5%, the effect will be falling prices and increasing purchasing power.

In the free market, if the commodity money became very valuable, that would give incentive for businesses to increase mining operations. Just like any product or service in the free market, the quantity of money would increase when entrepreneurs saw the mining of metals to be more profitable than other business ventures.

So the quantity of money would naturally take care of itself without the need for regulation. New forms of money would be open to entering the free market as well. For example, if our population grew substantially, then another, more plentiful metal would likely be incorporated into the monetary system, leaving silver for mid-range purchases and gold for luxury purchases.

Rather than borrow from the Federal Reserve, the government can just print its own debt-free money.
For many people who are aware of the problems with the Federal Reserve, this is the solution put forward: give total monetary control to the government and have their money creation be debt-free. While money which is not loaned into existence is better for the economy than money which is, the reliance on fiat money and government control has several fatal flaws which prevent me encouraging such a solution. The boom and bust business cycles are not dependent upon debt-based money, but just the creation of fiat currency and the manipulation of the interest rate. This approach would not prevent the inflationary booms and deflationary depressions. Essentially, this solution hinges on having extreme faith in government officials to keep the supply of money increasing only as fast as the supply of precious metals. Someone would have to be very naïve about the nature of government, and the history of government interference in the economy for its own benefit or for the benefit of select groups, in order to promote such a plan.

Beyond the argument from effect though, is the more fundamental reason I cannot support this approach. As we have gone over earlier, the government is simply a collection of individuals who have no special powers or rights and who do not respect the property rights of others. Governments are inherently unethical, and I would not support a monopoly of force to control any aspect of our lives, especially not one as important as money.

Rather than giving a small group of people control over the money supply of a country, region or the whole planet, the commodity-backed approach is as decentralized as you can get. No one has power over others. No one can control market-wide interest rates or easily increase or decrease the quantity of money.

Why waste resources and labor creating commodity-money when fiat money can be created almost for free? The resources which are not used can then go toward productive endeavors.

Of course we like to acquire goods as cheaply as possibly, but when the cost of producing money is next to nothing, the natural mechanism which prevents inflation is taken away. And as we went over earlier, an increase in the supply of money, unlike other goods, does not give any benefit to society. The costs of production are important price signals which tell people whether or not it is profitable to increase the supply. This acts to keep the quantity from inflating too quickly. While easy money and credit do free up capital, we saw that the money which inflation does not steal away from people tends to increase wasteful investments, which leads to a period of depression.

The Secrets to Nonviolent Prosperity

Chapter 4

TROUBLESOME TAXES

Man can live and satisfy his wants only by ceaseless labor; by ceaseless application of his faculties to natural resources. This process is the origin of property. But it is also true that a man may live and satisfy his wants by seizing and consuming the products of the labor of others. This process is the origin of plunder. Now since man is naturally inclined to avoid pain - and since labor is pain itself - it follows that men will resort to plunder whenever plunder is easier than work... When plunder becomes a way of life for a group of men living in society, they create for themselves, in the course of time, a legal system that authorizes it and a moral code that glorifies it.

Frederic Bastiat, *The Law*, 1850

In the several years of inflationary boom preceding the current depression, we saw housing prices dramatically increase. One consequence of this was sharply higher property taxes. *The Wall Street Journal* reported in February of 2005, that many people in the country were revolting against unfair property taxes. People who had purchased homes long ago, were being forced to pay substantially more in taxes due to the building frenzy around them, without having the better jobs with which to pay them. Even people who just bought a house a few years earlier saw their taxes raise so much that they decided to sue the tax assessor. Homeowners in Caanan, New York, saw their property taxes double over 10 years, residents in Harris County, Texas, which includes Houston, witnessed their property taxes go up over 106% in just 7 years, and property owners across Louisiana complained about tax assessment increases of between 100% and 500%, leading to a slew of lawsuits across the country (Smith, 2005).

WHAT'S THE PROBLEM?

You may not have thought about it before, but now that we have established the validity and importance of property rights, you can see that taxation is theft. Every time that you pay a tax, your property is either being taken by force or by the threat of force. Most people that I have talked to do not like paying taxes. People pay them for a few reasons: they haven't thought about the issue at all and just go along with what they are told to do; they do not think society could function without taxes; they feel it is their patriotic duty to pay their "fair share"; or they are afraid of the consequences of not paying.

All taxation is unethical because not all parties are involved voluntarily, and it is therefore a violation of property rights. The government does not like it when individuals and businesses do not pay taxes and will go after these people with fines and then imprisonment. But you probably already knew that, considering those are the very reasons most people are afraid of the Internal Revenue Service.

The services which these taxes go towards cannot really be called services since we are forced to pay for them. If we choose not to contribute to the service, then we will get notices, then fines, then threat of imprisonment, and ultimately, if we continue to resist, the barrel of a gun, which is what all government actions are backed up with. You can ask yourself if you would be willing to use violence against your neighbor to take money from him to pay for some service that he does not care for, like the libraries for example. Most people would not be willing to resort to violence, and yet they are willing to outsource this aggression to a third party called government.

> Today, nobody sees, or wishes to see, that in our time the enslavement of the majority of men is based on money taxes, levied on land and otherwise, which are collected by the government from subjects.
>
> Leo Tolstoy,
> Russian writer, 1891

> The metamorphosis of taxes into weapons of destruction is the mark of present-day public finance.
>
> Ludwig von Mises,
> *Human Action,* 1963

WHY ARE THERE TAXES?

There are two ways to acquire property: one can homestead, produce, contract or receive a gift, or one can steal from and exploit homesteaders, producers, contractors, and gift receivers. The latter is a downward spiral from prosperity to destitution. Both forms of property acquisition have been around for all of human history, but that does not make both of them ethical. While long ago taxes may have seemed more oppressive because they were obviously for the enrichment of the elite class, today those who impose taxes have cleverly chosen to get the good will of the masses on their side, touting the alleged benefits to society from

111

their tax-funded programs. It is this belief which sustains our tax system and allows the rate at which we are taxed to be so much higher than it was 100 years ago (approximately 5.9% average total tax rate in 1900; approximately 50% average total tax rate in 2009). People put up with, and even demand these taxes because many think that it is the only way to get certain needs met.

> A heavy progressive or graduated income tax.
>> 2nd Plank of communism,
>> *The Communist Manifesto*,
>> Karl Marx & Friedrich Engels, 1848

> Progressive taxation of income and profits means that precisely those parts of the income which people would have saved and invested are taxed away.
>> Ludwig von Mises,
>> *Economic Policy*, 1979

WHAT ARE THE CONSEQUENCES OF TAXATION?

The first consequence when a system of taxation is setup is the destruction of property rights. People no longer have full control over their property and cannot do with it as they please.

When someone is taxed, they are no longer able to use the property that was taken from them. This means they have less money with which to patronize businesses, invest or save. Each of these are key to a growing economy.

Taxes take money that would have gone to where people most valued it and puts it toward what people value less. How is this known? Because force is used. When someone has complete control over their property, they will use it in whatever ways they think are best. But when it is taken from them, the money can no longer go to those places.

> I believe in only one thing: liberty... The state I care nothing for. All the state has ever meant to me is unjust taxation... A good writer will never like the government he lives under. His hand should be against it and its hand will always be against him.
>
> Ernest Hemingway,
> American writer, 1935

If the government's use of the money would be the same as what each person would have spent their money on, then taxes would be unnecessary. This means that taxes shift the supply and demand in the economy from certain industries which people would have patronized to others which they were forced to support, including paying the salaries of the bureaucrats themselves.

To use an argument from philosopher Stefan Molyneux, if a majority of people are good, then they would want to contribute to programs which help people out anyway, and if the majority is bad, then bad people would be in control of a coercive monopoly. In any case, government and taxes are unnecessary.

> With courage and prudence, a man can protect himself from illegal plunder, but no one can escape from legal plunder. If someone tries, what is the distressing spectacle presented to society? A plunderer armed with the law, a victim resisting the law.
>
> Frederic Bastiat,
> French economist, 1848

Below is a partial list of the various taxes that those in the United States pay:

Accounts Receivable Tax, Building Permit Tax, Capital Gains Tax, Commercial Driver's License Tax, Cigarette Tax, Corporate Income Tax, Court Fines (indirect taxes), Deficit spending, Dog License Tax, Federal Income Tax, Federal Unemployment Tax, Fishing License Tax, Food License Tax, Fuel permit tax, Gasoline Tax, Hunting License Tax, Inflation, Inheritance Tax Interest expense (tax on the money), Inventory tax IRS Interest Charges (tax on top of tax), IRS Penalties (tax on top of tax), Liquor Tax, Local Income Tax, Luxury Taxes, Marriage License Tax, Medicare Tax, Property Tax, Real Estate Tax, Septic Permit Tax, Service Charge Taxes, Social Security Tax, Road Usage Taxes (Truckers), Sales Taxes, Recreational Vehicle Tax, Road Toll Booth Taxes, School Tax, State Income Tax, State Unemployment Tax, Telephone federal excise tax, Telephone federal universal service fee tax, Telephone federal, state and local surcharge taxes, Telephone minimum usage surcharge tax, Telephone recurring and non-recurring charges tax, Telephone state and local tax, Telephone usage charge tax, Toll Bridge Taxes, Toll Tunnel Taxes, Trailer Registration Tax, Utility Taxes, Vehicle License Registration Tax, Vehicle Sales Tax, Watercraft Registration Tax, Well Permit Tax, and Workers Compensation Tax.

The income tax is intimately connected to the Federal Reserve Banking system. The system uses "withholding" (income which is withheld by one's employer to pay taxes) to absorb escalating inflation, conceal currency devaluation and prevent people from spending all that they earn.

Escalating taxes on productivity penalizes those who are most financially successful. Rather than being rewarded for creating a product or service that so many people are choosing to give their money in exchange for, they have more of their money taken away. This is a disincentive to be productive, leading to a less productive economy.

While most people do not like paying taxes, they think that the economy and society would collapse without them. Many people believe that we would no longer have an educational system, roads being built or have our food quality regulated. Fortunately, the success of an economy is not dependent on having taxes. These services would absolutely be provided in a free market, as they were before being taken over by the government. And with the introduction of competition the quality would increase while the costs would fall - a wonderful thing for us all. In the free enterprise system, no one would be forced to work for the benefit of another (sometimes known as slavery) and no other person could expect to have that person work for him.

It is ridiculous to assert that rational men would fail to voluntarily support services they need if they were not forced to do so. And it is ridiculous, as well as unethical, to force men to support services they do not use and do not value, just because a select group think they know what is best for everybody else.

> It probably is not necessary for the federal government to tax anyone directly; it could simply print the money it needs. However, that would be too bold a stroke, for it would then be obvious to all what kind of counterfeiting operation the government is running. The present system combining taxation and inflation is akin to watering the milk; too much water and the people catch on.
> Ron Paul,
> U.S. Congressman, 1979

DIFFERENCES BETWEEN GOVERNMENT AND BUSINESS

What are the limits to business growth in a free market? A business can expand as long as it can attract new customers and keep its current ones. It does this in a number of different ways, including product innovation and competitive prices. If a customer is no longer satisfied with the services they are receiving, they can choose to stop patronizing the business and go to a competitor. Businesses that want to grow will try to serve their customers better than their competitors, resulting in better goods for lower prices.

What are the limits to government growth? Government expands through ever increasing taxation, some of which is overt, such as the income tax, and some of which is hidden, such as the "tax" through inflation.

> I regard government action and voluntary market action as diametrically opposite, the former necessarily involving violence, aggression and exploitation, and the latter being necessarily harmonious, peaceful and mutually beneficial for all.
>
> Murray Rothbard, American
> philosopher and economist, 1969

Unlike business growth, government growth does not cause prosperity for the people. Though often times both prosperity and taxation will go up over a given period of time, this enhanced living standard is in spite of the taxation, not because of it. What limits the growth of taxes, and therefore government, is public opinion. If the theft is too extreme, the people will rebel, so the people have to be deceived into believing that the taxes are good for them.

In the 20th century, a major ideological shift occurred, where the government size greatly expanded on the idea that they should not just provide protection of private property, but that they should be involved in every aspect of people's lives, from birth to death. Slowly, people forgot that government was not always responsible for everything in their lives, such as education, health care, roads, social security, etc. People thus became dependent on the government, and saw only government as the solution to their various problems.

I want to recognize how difficult it can be to envision a world in which government is not so thoroughly involved in our affairs, much less a world where there are no geographical monopolies on force, where violent means are not used to solve social problems. When we grow up with government all around us, it can be a challenge to think that a truly free society is possible. Many people think the government is like air - it is everywhere and we need it to survive. The first part is true, that it is everywhere, but we certainly do not need it to survive. In fact, government is more like a parasite since its only means of survival is by living off of the people by coercively extracting their wealth. This parasite has tricked us into thinking that our well-being is dependent upon it. When we allow ourselves to stop breathing in this parasitic "air" and challenge our current system, we can then open ourselves up to the possibilities of real peace and prosperity. Considering the dismal state of our economy, there is no better time than now to begin questioning our assumptions about the place of government in our lives.

THE DAWN OF GLOBAL TAXES

Over the years taxes have expanded from just local to state, to national, and now global. The United Nations has proposed global taxes which would be a worldwide program for redistributing wealth away from those who have worked hard for it. Just because some people make agreements, which supposedly bind the masses to follow their dictates, does not make them ethical. Once again it comes back to protecting your own property and not allowing others, whether individuals or groups, whether big or small, to claim a right to take what is yours.

I Object!
Answers to Common Questions and Objections

We can't have civilization without taxes
Civilization is built not on legalized plunder and forced redistribution of wealth but rather on the protection of people's property. It is this protection which allows people to keep the fruits of their labor, a key incentive for innovating and creating products and services for the marketplace. Taxes do not create what a society most wants, but what the politicians want.

> You compare the nation to a parched piece of land, and the tax to a life-giving rain. So be it. But you should ask yourself where this rain comes from, and whether it is precisely the tax that draws the moisture from the soil and dries it up.
>
> Frederic Bastiat,
> French economist, 1850

> It is a glaring absurdity to pretend that taxation contributes to national wealth, by engrossing part of the national produce, and enriches the nation by consuming part of its wealth. Indeed, it would be trifling with my reader's time, to notice such a fallacy, did not most governments act upon this

principle, and had not well intentioned and scientific writers endeavored to support and establish it.

Jean-Baptiste Say,
French economist, 1821

What about the poor and the disadvantaged?

While the purpose of ethical laws is to protect people's property, there is never a lack of those who wish to distort it and use the law for false philanthropy. The poor, uneducated and generally disadvantaged are easy targets because most people care about the well-being of others. Real philanthropy, mutual-aid organizations and businesses could take care of the needs of these people, but calls for tax-funded programs simply mean that you want to forcefully take money from people. It is a sad state when we believe that the only way to care for some people is to violate others.

If people's taxes were to be eliminated each person would be significantly wealthier and individual giving would likely go up. Many believe that while they would contribute to programs to care for people, others are not so thoughtful and generous. Most of the people I have talked with hold this belief. In truth, caring for others is not unique to one or a few people; the great majority of people really care about the well-being of people in general and would take some sort of action to help out those in need. In fact, if enough people care about the poor to have laws passed, then the laws to not need to be passed because the large number of people who would be voting for the law could just take direct action to aid those in need, bypassing the government altogether.

It's amazing to me how many people think that voting to have the government give poor people money is compassion. Helping poor and suffering people yourself is compassion. Voting for our government to use guns to give money to help poor and suffering people is immoral self-righteous bullying laziness. People need to be fed, medicated, educated, clothed, and sheltered. If We're compassionate, we'll help them, but you get no moral credit for forcing other people to do what you think is right. There is great joy in helping people, but no joy in doing it at gunpoint.

Penn Jillette,
American magician, 2009

We do not need to hear calls for "free" education, universal healthcare, welfare and social security. All of these services can be provided on the free market without the need for taxes and the involuntary redistribution of wealth. Real philanthropy is when you work for your money and give some away voluntarily. False philanthropy is when you legally steal money from people and give it to others.

Fair Shares and Free Rides

There is a common concern that those who do not pay their "fair share" are getting a "free ride" on the backs of the tax-payers. Those not paying get the benefit of tax-funded roads, emergency services, parks, libraries, etc. In our current society, this makes perfect sense. But remember, socialism is based on taking away people's property and giving it to others - legalized plunder.

If we look at this situation with an understanding of property rights, the true problems become apparent and they clear up immediately. In the free market there would be no government-owned parks, libraries, educational system or emergency services. These services would of course be provided in the free market because many people value them, but their funds would come only from those who voluntarily gave money to them.

One of the primary goals of this book is to show people that violence is not a necessary means to get the programs and products that we value. In the same way that taking property from people against their will is unnecessary in order to bring computers, cars and coffee to market, the same is true of goods which are currently funded by taxes. If people value them, then they will be provided on the free market, most likely in a form which is even more satisfying to the consumer. "Free riders" and paying one's "fair share" are not important concepts in a free market because people get what they pay for.

Taxes are ethical as long as they are voted on

Many believe that while a tax imposed by a king would be unethical, a tax approved by a majority of voters would be ethical. A tax is a tax though, whether brought about by an individual or a group of people in the majority. It is important to note that a vote taking place to determine whether people's property should be plundered is *already violating the property rights of the individuals*. Why? Because the very act of voting means that you think rights are negotiable, and the larger group can determine what those rights are. Therefore each person has their true rights violated when voting takes place. So even the vote that supposedly legitimizes a new tax is itself unethical. The only way a tax would be ethical would be if every person who would be paying, approved of having a tax and the amount they would pay. At that point it would be a voluntary contribution, not a tax. Majority voting does not make legislation voluntary. It doesn't matter if 99% of the population is in favor of a progressive income tax, the 1% are still being coerced, like the majority in a lynch-mob which takes the rights away from the unfortunate minority.

121

Legislation is not the result of consensus. If there were a consensus there would be no need for legislation. Legislation represents civil war.

Leonard Liggio,
American law professor, 1983

What then is legislation? ...It is the assumption by one man, or a body of men, of a right to abolish outright all the natural rights, all the natural liberty of all other men; to make all other men their slaves; to arbitrarily dictate to all other men what they may, and may not, do; what they may, and may not, be. It is, in short, the assumption of a right to banish the principle of human rights, the principle of justice itself, from off the earth, and set up their own personal will, pleasure and interest in its place. All this, and nothing less, is involved in the very idea that there can be any such thing as human legislation that is obligatory upon those upon whom it is imposed.

Lysander Spooner,
American philosopher, 1882

Chapter 5

DIRTY WORDS

No, this is not a chapter about four-letter profanities, but a different class of words that are equally reviled by many people. These often bring up such intense emotions that they may even be considered worse than those prohibited in school. This chapter takes a close look at some of those words, breaking down the misconceptions, and showing their true value. The second part of this chapter is about those words and phrases which do not typically spark an emotional reaction, but if you have understood the principles thus far, they likely will.

It's time to take off the ear-muffs!

Profit

While most people are happy to hear their child made a profit on the lemonade stand, many are not so enthusiastic when the profit is made by a big business. The perception is that corporate fat-cats are ripping off the consumers and unjustly making huge sums. While there are numerous examples of people who's wealth has been greatly increased due to subsidies, legislation and government contracts, that is a problem not of profit but of government intervention in the market process.

The truth is that profits are the lifeblood of any business, and thus of the whole economy. If a business is not profitable, then it will eventually cease to exist. If you look around you right now, you will see many things: this book, maybe a house or building, clothes, cars, food, etc. You are able to get all of these goods because the businesses were profitable.

> An economy is like a living organism and grows and contracts as it is fed or starved. The food for a healthy economy is incentive, because incentive is what makes it worthwhile for people to be imaginative and enterprising, which will in turn cause the economy to expand.
>
> Jennifer Roback,
> American economist, 1981

Let's take a closer look at what a profit actually is. If you go to a store and buy some pieces of plastic for $1, then configure them in a way where people will buy it for $10, then you will have made approximately $9 in profit. What really happened was that you took something that anybody could get for $1 and turned it into something that many people valued for more than 10 times that amount. And this is what profits are all about. Wherever profit rates are greatest in the free market, it shows where people most valued the finished products over the resources used to create them. As other entrepreneurs enter the field, the quality of the products will increase as each company tries to differentiate itself and win over customers. Costs will decrease as production becomes more efficient and the price to the consumer will go down due to competition.

A profit is only bad when it was acquired through force or deception, in which case the money was simply stolen. For ethical business practices though, the only way that big profits can be obtained is through pleasing the customer. A business would not succeed if the consumers did not think that the products or services were of more value to them than the money they would give up in exchange.

There is another interesting way to look at profits: the value that the customers received from a business with $10 billion in revenue actually exceeded $10 billion! People only purchase products or services if they believe that they will value them *more* than the money they cost. If we say that the profit rate is 10%, then the business owners get $1 billion in profit, while the customers received more than $10 billion in value.

> There would not be any profits but for the eagerness of the public to acquire the merchandise offered for sale by the successful entrepreneur. But the same people who scramble for these articles vilify the businessman and call his profit ill-got. One of the main functions of profit is to shift the control of capital to those who know how to employ it in the best possible way for the satisfaction of the public.
>
> Ludwig von Mises,
> Austrian economist, 1952

As you can see, profit is a big part of what makes an economy prosper. In a free market, when we would hear a report about a company's massive profits, we could think about how many people's lives were enriched, and maybe even be inspired to seek out some more profits for ourselves. Unfortunately, our current economy has substantial government intervention which makes people rightly skeptical of the profits of some companies. It can sometimes be hard to know if a business earned those profits or was a beneficiary of legislation.

CHARGING INTEREST

Charging interest on a loan is often seen as gouging the borrower. Throughout the ages, those who charged interest were looked down upon as scoundrels. This comes from the idea that people shouldn't get something for nothing. If someone loans out money, they aren't doing anything, but they end up with more money than when they started.

Let's look more closely at what interest is, and whether or not charging it is ethical.

When someone has money, they are able to use it to satisfy their present needs or to build more capital by investing it. The person could take the cash and loan it out or use it to build a store, for example. If the person loans the money, they must forego the use of it and therefore cannot profit off of the new store. Thus, if someone is going to loan money, they must see that they will get more value from it than using it themselves.

If I want to go into business but don't have the money, I will need to borrow. I will be willing to pay the interest rate if I have figured that I will be financially rewarded for taking this risk. Think of interest as rent paid on money. If you are renting an apartment, you pay for your use of it. You give the owner regular payments, and when the contract is expired, you give back the apartment as well. A loan is simply rented money and the interest is the rental fee.

Money is worth more to people in the present than in the future, and that is why people are willing to pay the premium of interest on a loan in order to have the money in the present.

Just like with other goods, money goes to where it is most valued. If a businessperson has a great idea which he believes will be very successful, he will be willing to pay interest on a loan. And thus the money will go from the investor to the businessman, where it will potentially grow more quickly.

Turning our attention to modern banking, we run into a problem. As we have seen here, charging interest on loans is ethical because you are simply renting out your money for a period of time. Most modern loans are not ethical, but this is not due to the banks charging interest.

The problem with modern banking is that they use fiat currency, and they have very low reserve ratios. What does this mean? They are charging interest on money that doesn't really exist. A low reserve ratio, say 10%, means that your $1 deposit in the bank can magically be turned into $10 in loans. The banks then charge interest on the money they just created with a few entries into the computer. In this case interest charges are not ethical, but only because of the foundation of fiat currency and fractional-reserve banking.

MONOPOLY

Cool board-game, frightening word for many people. It conjures up images of a big, bad company squashing all of the little ones, gouging the consumers and becoming all powerful. This company would come to control the resources vital to people's survival and would then be able to force people to do their bidding in return for rationed resources. What a picture.

In order to understand monopolies, we need first to understand free competition. The meaning of free competition is that every industry and occupation would be legally open to anyone who deems that they are equipped to succeed and wish to try and the buyers would be free to choose among them. That sounds simple enough.

The political concept of monopoly states that a monopoly is a market, or part of a market, reserved to the exclusive possession of one or more sellers by means of the initiation of force by government, or with the sanction of the government.

> It is a grotesque distortion of the true state of affairs to speak of monopoly capitalism instead of monopoly interventionism, and of private cartels instead of government-made cartels.
>
> Ludwig von Mises,
> Austrian economist, 1949

A monopoly exists only when freedom of competition is violated. Though it may cost $500 million in capital expenditures to establish one's business in certain high-cost industries, that does not mean the industry is acting in a monopolistic way. If you could find a cheaper way to compete, you would be free to do so. Since no one is imposing the costs on you in order to enter the industry, but rather they are capital requirements needed to compete, they do not violate freedom of competition.

While the government has some monopolies which it runs, like the Post Office (first class mail), and the government schooling system (more on that shortly), many of the monopolies that exist are through the licensing laws the government enacts which forcefully shut out from the marketplace those who are not license holders. Examples of license monopolies are: lawyers, dentists, barbers, massage therapists, contractors, liquor store owners, psychologists, teachers, accountants, opticians and taxi cab drivers and many more. These laws result in a decreased supply of workers in these industries, which drive up the prices. Monopolies exist, and freedom of competition is violated, not when one seller exists in a market when all are free to enter, but when many sellers are in a market and some, who would normally be able to compete, are barred entry.

> Institute for Justice client Mike Rife, of Texas, cannot compete with a government-created cartel that demands he close his businesses and complete a three-year apprenticeship under a licensed private investigator to get a state-required license to fix computers.
>
> Institute for Justice, 2008

Since 1937, the number of taxi cabs that are allowed to cruise the streets in New York City has been forcibly limited to a little under 12,000. In order for people to become taxi cab drivers there, they must get a small metal medallion, issued by the city. Because of the limited supply of medallions, they can sell for over $100,000 each. Normally if someone is a good driver, knows the area and has a car, they could start taxiing people around, but the price for the medallions prevents many people from becoming drivers. This artificial stunting of the supply of taxi cab drivers increases the price that consumers pay. With more competition those prices would go down and the quality would go up.

Minimum-wage and pro-union legislation act to reserve a portion of the job market to a reduced number of employees at greater wage rates. In these cases, those who are not worth the minimum-wage to an employer, or are not part of a union, will not be employed. These laws protect the more skilled workers and prevent a huge number of people from becoming productive employees. As the minimum-wage goes higher and as union benefits increase, the protected class becomes smaller and the disadvantaged class becomes bigger. The reason minimum-wage laws, pro-union legislation and tariffs exist is to benefit those in the protected class.

Those in unions join because they believe their situation will be improved. Fortunately there are nonviolent means to attain increasing levels of prosperity. On the free market, unions could still exist, and they would be able use persuasion when talking with the owner and they could also strike en masse. They would not be allowed to physically prevent anyone from going to work, use violence against person or property, and they could not force contract compromises on the owner.

Antitrust lawsuits, which are supposedly to protect consumers, are almost never brought against a company by them, but rather by the competitors. The consumers often benefit when a company gets big because they take advantage of economies of scale and pass much of the savings on to the consumers.

As long as one company does not use force against another to prevent its entry into the field, then there is not a problem. The activities prohibited by antitrust legislation are peaceful ones, and whether they result in increased or decreased efficiency, they should be allowed in a free market.

Many people are concerned that if a company has a large percentage of the market, then that company will pump up its prices and rip everyone off. This concern is especially important when it comes to a company dominating the supplies of a vital resource, such as oil, water or food. However, this flies in the face of supply and demand. If the company raised its prices substantially, two things would happen. First, the company would lose customers who were not willing to pay the higher rate. Second, entrepreneurs would see the profit being made and enter the industry. The new businesses would be able to offer the product at a lower price and thus capture some of the market. In order for the bigger company to keep its sales up, it would have to lower its prices every time there was a competitor who was undercutting them. If the public saw a pattern of the company jacking up the prices when there wasn't competition, they would lose trust in the company and give their business to the competing start-ups which offered the lower prices and showed more integrity.

Monopolies simply do not exist unless they are created, protected and/or subsidized by a government. People will only continue to support a business as long as they think they are getting more value than they are giving away in the form of money. As contradictory as it may be to what you have thought, *antitrust legislation actually encourages government-protected monopoly*. Why? Because it is interfering with a market in which people are free to leave and enter at their will, and in which the buyers are free to choose from whom they will buy, and giving benefits to the less efficient businesses at the cost of more efficient ones. When government gives benefits to a certain group, they are a government-protected monopoly.

Rather than a company earning its way to the top of the market-share in a given industry, this legislation encourages less efficient ones to sue the big, successful businesses in order to hamper their productivity and give themselves a leg-up. If companies had to make it the honest way, then they would do so by creating products which are significantly better and/or prices which are significantly lower than the leader, causing people to patronize their business. The free market is the spontaneous harmony of interests and leads to more creativity, better products and lower prices. A win for everyone except those who are currently protected.

> The entire structure of antitrust statutes in this country is a jumble of economic irrationality and

ignorance. It is the product: (a) of a gross misinterpretation of history, and (b) of rather naïve, and certainly unrealistic economic theories... No one will ever know what new products, processes, machines, and cost saving mergers failed to come into existence, killed by the Sherman Act before they were born. No one can compute the price that all of us have paid for that Act which, by inducing the less effective use of capital, has kept our standard of living lower than would have otherwise been possible. No speculation, however, is required, to assess the injustice and the damage to the careers, reputations, and lives of business executives jailed under the antitrust laws.

Alan Greenspan, Federal Reserve Chairman, 1961,
before his government tenure

This brings us back to the point that consumers are not the ones who are hurt by companies with large shares of the market. They are able to get quality products at a discounted rate. This is bad for their competitors however. So the competitors, instead of trying to grow their customer base by lowering their price or making a superior product, choose to go to the government and ask for force to be used against the successful company to make the playing field "fair".

The sole source of the monopoly power, and of the problem, is the state. Yet it is the very state that most of the critics of business (and supporters of antitrust) would expand and enlarge to suit their particular vision of the good society. Knowingly or unknowingly, the critics of big business would enhance the very institution, and the very relationships that are at the root of the social problem they claim to abhor.

Dominick T. Armentano,
American economist, 1972

While many of the monopolies which exist are the licensing and tariff sort, there are also government-owned and government-subsidized monopolies. For example, the United States Postal Service prevents competition in certain categories, such as first class mail, in which FedEx and UPS would certainly enjoy being allowed to compete.

The public school system is a massive government monopoly (a topic which really deserves an entire book unto itself). Because government schools are able to charge the customers below cost - nothing for elementary through high school and minimal for city colleges - they gain an unfair advantage over the competition. Unless parents want to pay twice for their child to attend a private school - first in taxes, then again in tuition - they attend a public school. What happens when there is a government enforced monopoly? Prices go up and quality goes down. What have we seen with public schools? Exactly. The public school system is a money pit, with the schools claiming that all they need is more money, but over the years as more and more money has come in, educational quality has gone down. Current private schools are not the free market answer as they have to comply with educational standards set by the governments.

The education of all children, from the moment they can get along without a mother's care, shall be in state institutions at state expense.

Karl Marx & Friedrich Engels,
The Communist Manifesto, 1848

> A general State education is a mere contrivance for moulding people to be exactly alike one another; and as the mould in which it casts them is that which pleases the predominant power in the government, whether this be a monarch, a priesthood, an aristocracy, or the majority of the existing generation; in proportion as it is efficient and successful, it establishes despotism over the mind, leading by a natural tendency to one over the body.
>
> John Stuart Mill,
> British philosopher, 1859

The low quality and high cost of government education is due to the lack of competition. When you have an audience that is forced to use your services, there is little incentive to improve the quality. As soon as competition is introduced, the new schools do not automatically get the local children to come to their school, they have to appeal to the parents by offering something better or cheaper than their competitors.

> It was the wine of error that was presented to us in our childhood by our inebriated teachers; they punished us when we refused to drink of it, and we could not appeal from their sentence to any judge who was not as drunk as they.
>
> Saint Augustine, 354-430 A.D.

If you don't like the service of the dominant company, patronize a competitor. If there aren't any, then you can start up a competing business because your dissatisfaction is probably not unique. While this may not be easy, a good idea combined with ambition certainly makes it possible.

If people are truly concerned about the effects of a monopoly, then rather than using government to break up companies, people should be concerned with the largest monopoly of all, government itself. Government is a monopoly of force within a claimed territory. And if there is one monopoly that we should be opposed to, it is this one, not worrying about what percentage of the online search market Google has.

CONSUMERISM

This is a word used to describe what is often regarded as a disease - people choosing to purchase more than what is needed to survive.

The claim is that these people, in reality the vast majority, are destroying the planet by buying too many products. It is believed that we are being seduced by advertising into exchanging non-renewable resources for consumer products which are mostly unnecessary. The primary fear is that while we may be enjoying an era of plenty now, we are only able to live this way by using up our future resources, which will inevitably run out; and because our population is rapidly growing, there will be a massive die off. I was taught this belief during my environmental   science classes, so I can sympathize with the emotions associated with that perspective.

> Few arguments are more dangerous than the one's which "feel" right but can't be justified.
>
> Stephen Jay Gould,
> *The Mismeasure of Man*, 1981

Further, they hold that our continually increasing consumption levels led to pollution, resource depletion and social problems, all while not satisfying our real, higher-order needs, such as relationships, achievements and personal growth. What they have been led to believe is the free market is to blame because it gives the power to producers, which can manipulate the consumers into purchasing products we don't really want or need. To the person making the judgements, the consumed items are always unnecessary. But for the people making the purchases, they are valuing those goods over the money they gave up for them. There is no master list of what people should spend their money on. People have different values, and their money gets allocated accordingly.

> We cannot long continue our present rate of progress.
>
> W. Stanley Jevons,
> British economist, 1865

> We have timber for less than 30 years...coal for but 50 years.
>
> Gifford Pinchot,
> *The Fight for Conservation*, 1910

Let me first recognize that this set of conservation beliefs really comes from a good place for most people. It often stems from a concern for humanity's future well-being, making sure we have enough food, clean water, and natural beauty for generations to come.

Fortunately, we humans are amazing at being able to come up with ways to more efficiently use the resources we have as well as continually find more. All of the resources have become more plentiful over time, particularly during the past 150 years. As we use up resources which are most easily accessible we then resort to resources which are more costly to acquire. Technological advances can make previously expensive resources far less so. It seems pretty obvious that our resources are finite considering we are on living on a sphere floating through space. But the amount of energy, chemicals and resources that are contained within this planet are so massive as to be virtually infinite. It is human ingenuity which transforms these elements into things which we desire more, such as houses, appliances, food, automobiles, and even the roads and trails we use to get away from it all and appreciate the natural beauty.

Some may be concerned about the plentitude of such resources as clean water, soil and oil. It is important to recognize that while there may be shortages, this is not due to something inherent in the resources or the free market. In fact, these shortages only occur when there is government intervention in the market. The price system is critical to having our resources be sustainable because it shows us how valuable the resources are on the market. If subsidies conceal the true cost, then these resources can become used up. I certainly do not want to give the impression that we can just sit back and there will always be plentiful resources. It is the free market which allows for maximum efficiency in production and in finding new resources. If governments get in the way of this, there is no guarantee that we won't run out of clean water, oil or any other resource.

One effective way to tell if the supply of resources is increasing or decreasing is by looking at their prices over time. As something becomes more scarce, its price goes up, and when it becomes more plentiful, the price goes down. In 1980, economist Julian Simon made a $10,000 bet with Stanford University environmentalists Ehrlich, Harte and Holden as to whether prices of specified resources would go up or down. The doomsayer environmentalists believed that we were running out of resources, so they predicted prices of chromium, copper, nickel, tin and tungsten would go up over the course of 10 years. In September of 1990, the new prices, adjusted for inflation, were recorded, showing a collective decrease for the whole basket of resources as well as a decrease in each individual item. The environmentalists did not just pick the "wrong" resources on which to wager however, because all resources had become cheaper, including petroleum, minerals, sugar, wool, cotton and foodstuffs. Julian Simon put his money where his mouth was and won the bet. Unfortunately, many people are still under the delusion that our resource levels are static and finite.

> Our supplies of natural resources are not finite in any economic sense. Nor does past experience give reason to expect natural resources to become more scarce. Rather, if history is any guide, natural resources will progressively become less costly, hence less scarce, and will constitute a smaller proportion of our expenses in future years.
>
> Julian Simon,
> *The Ultimate Resource 2,* 1981

It is people's confusion about the near infinitude of resources and lack of basic economic understanding which leads to the mentality that we *need* to recycle. If a business can make a new product using fewer workers and resources than it would take to make the good out of recycled products, then it makes sense to create new ones. In fact, resources would be *wasted* if the business was compelled to use recycled materials. If it is more profitable for a business to make their products from recycled material, they will do so voluntarily, and they would actually pay people for their recycled goods as opposed to us paying to have them taken away. This is already very common among industries, where one business purchases the wastes of other businesses and makes them into new products. When people pay more for products which are made from recycled materials because they believe that we are running out of resources and it is good for the planet, the effect is to patronize less efficient methods of satisfying people's needs. The extra money that is spent on those items cannot be spent on others, which means that other industries have to shrink, lowering our overall productivity. It is interesting to note that the lower productive efficiency actually takes more resources to satisfy people's needs.

Some people may be concerned about running out of space to put all of the waste. Fortunately, this is another concern that the free market can easily take care of. The key is the price system. If it is more expensive to have land dedicated to be landfill sites than it would be to recycle those materials, then businesses will naturally choose to recycle. While the media makes it seem as if we are running out of places to put garbage because they show video of overflowing landfills, the problem is the severely limited number of new sites that the government allows to be opened. There is plenty of completely unused and low value land that could be allocated for landfill sites, and nobody would ever think there was a problem again.

One of the great things about humans is the ability to be creative beyond the need for survival. Music, art, skyscrapers and airplanes are not necessary for our survival, but they sure do enrich many people's lives.

CAPITALISM

This word shows up a lot in the media, often considered to be a virus that is devouring the earth. Most people's views are that capitalism is a system of exploitation whereby the rich can force the poor to do their bidding. The term was created by socialists not to educate, but to condemn, and today it has become a political catchword where its mere utterance can stir up people's hostility. Yes, for many this is a truly hated word.

Unfortunately, capitalism is severely misunderstood.

Capitalism is very simple; it is the voluntary exchange of goods and services while respecting one another's property rights. Each person owns resources, even if just one's body, and is able to use them in trade. People are able to choose how they want to live and what interests they wish to pursue. They are not forced at all. Capitalism is characterized by the pursuit of material and/or non-material well-being under freedom and the harmony of self-interests of each of those involved. In this system, the individual is legally free from the initiation of physical force. This means that no law would support the initiation of force against someone.

> Capitalism is not simply mass production, but mass production to satisfy the needs of the masses. The arts and crafts of the good old days catered almost exclusively to the wants of the well-to-do. But the factories produce cheap goods for the many. Big business, the target of fanatical hatred on the part of all contemporary governments and self-styled intellectuals, acquired and preserved its business only because it works for the masses.
>
> Ludwig von Mises,
> Austrian economist, 1958

You may be concerned about the forced labor factories in different parts of the world. This is the very opposite of capitalism. Communist or socialist governments would promote forced labor, but not a true capitalist society. It is true that some companies take advantage of the low prices they are able to get by government-forced labor, and it is both dangerous and unethical when communist governments are supported by corporations. Just because a company seeks to maximize profits does not mean they are engaged in capitalism. For this to occur, all exchanges must be voluntary and property rights must be respected. In a society where people are able to make free choices about their occupation, those who choose to work in a factory do so because they believe it is their best option for improving their lives.

As people become confused about and afraid of capitalism, the level of our prosperity diminishes. This occurs because capitalism is what is responsible for vital economic growth around the world, and for our elevated living standard. When we turn our backs to capitalism by demanding more government intervention and by becoming more self-sufficient, our living standard becomes lower than what they would have been.

The increasing level of prosperity that has occurred during the past century will not continue on inevitably. We must be aware of what leads to a thriving economy. Let's be very clear about what capitalism is, reject all forms of forced labor, and embrace that which allows us to meet our needs and desires, peacefully. So next time you hear or read about capitalism, try to distinguish between what is the result of force and what is the result of voluntary exchange.

WORDS THAT SHOULD BE DIRTY

There are also some words which we should be more critical of when we hear them. Below are a few words or phrases that are vital for us to understand more deeply.

ECONOMIC STIMULUS PACKAGE

Politicians spout this phrase off left and right when the economy is slowing down. Of course the public wants the economy to be going stronger. Even in great times, people want it to be better. Many people are lured in by the idea that government can stimulate the economy, and the average person doesn't have to do anything. They just wait for prosperity to start raining down on them.

And so the politicians compete with one another on who can deliver the biggest package to the public, all the while not talking about, or minimizing, where it is coming from - the tax-paying public.

The truth is that government can never take action which stimulates the economy without dire consequences, whether in the short or long term. What they can do is stop their actions which are inhibiting the economy, which is all of them.

How do they propose to kick-start this growth? With lower interest rates and more money in circulation in the form of bailouts, subsidies and government programs. This is exactly the opposite of what is needed. More money and low interest rates lead to inflation, which devalues the currency and destroys an economy.

So whenever you hear someone talking about an economic stimulus package, be wary. And don't fall for the bait of their easy cure-alls.

"Free"

I mean this in the context of government services which are advertised to the public as being free: schooling, roads, parks, healthcare, libraries, roads, etc.

There is great allure to this word, and many in the business world have used it effectively to get new customers. But when it comes to government services, the truth is that they are all paid for through taxes or inflation, whether those affected like it or not.

Going back to the public libraries example, many people were exclaiming that libraries and information should be free, that they should not be privatized because people will just try to make a profit. All the desire for "free" government services really means is that people will not pay directly, but rather be forced to pay through taxes. It is hard to claim that something is free, when tax-payers are forced to pay hundreds and even thousands of dollars a year, whether or not they use the service. And if someone chooses not to pay, they will be taken to jail, or shot if they resist going.

People need to understand that when it comes to government, free is never an accurate word because government and its programs only survive because of the taxes they extract from people. So whenever you hear "free" in a government context, be aware that you will be paying for the service in the form of taxes or inflation.

Democracy

Democracy is not the wonderful political institution that many have been led to believe.

It should be clear from the *Rights All A Jumble* chapter that rights cannot be aggregated and thus pull more weight when large numbers of people are involved. When the politicians talk about bringing democracy to people, what they are doing is setting up an institution whereby some people have power over others.

> The current doctrine that private rights must yield to the public good, amounts in reality, to nothing more nor less than this, that an individual, or a minority, must consent to have less than their rights, in order that other individuals, or the majority, may have more than their rights.
>
> Lysander Spooner,
> American philosopher, 1860

This is often portrayed as bringing freedom to these people, however just the opposite is the result of a democracy. If freedom was truly the intention, then a system of property rights protection would be set up, thus allowing people to do what they like with their own property, so long as they do not aggress against others. But the first thing any form of government does is reject property rights by taking people's money against their will.

But what about doing things for the "common good"? These are things which benefit the community, like a school, park, hospital, water, etc. The free market can easily satisfy all of these needs. The problem with the "common good" ideology is that the majority who subscribe to this belief can completely undermine property rights for the rest of the people. For example, say the community decides they want to have a school where your house resides. Rather than just being outvoted or asked to just suck it up for the community good, a voluntary system would allow you to accept or reject arguments and/or monetary offers for your property.

To be more clear about the inherent problems with the one-person-one-vote system, imagine a small group of people who are being persecuted because they do not hold the religious beliefs of the majority. They in no way initiate aggression, but the majority group decides to have a vote with everyone, including the minority (how nice to include them!), as to wether or not these people should be forced to vacate their property. If the minority does not wish to participate, they get outvoted and the majority feels justified in taking action. If, on the other hand, the minority believes in democracy and chooses to participate, then they will get their own votes but will still be outvoted and forced to leave their land.

Even though Hitler was voted into power, that did not give him any moral ground to kill the Jews. In the same way, the majority in a lynch mob does not give their actions of lynching another human being any moral sanction.

> So long as we admit that the property of individuals lies at the mercy of the largest number of votes, we are intellectually and morally committed to state socialism.
>
> Auberon Herbert,
> English philosopher, 1897

The results of the majority believing the fallacy that rights can be aggregated is the same no matter what the minority chooses. Until property rights are respected, minorities will continue to get the short end of the stick.

Country/Nation

We are brought up from a young age to identify the squiggly shapes on a world map as countries. Many people feel strong loyalty to the country in which they grew up, and appreciate traveling the world exploring the many different territories.

However, there is a big difference between the land you grew up on and the country you grew up in. From space, you can see the land and the oceans of the world but you cannot see any lines making up the borders of countries. This is because our environment exists naturally while countries only exist in people's imagination.

When you look at a map and see the colors representing different countries, what you are seeing are the borders of various tax-farms. When someone says he is from the United States, Greece, China or any other country, what he is identifying is the government he lives under and to which he pays taxes.

Despite what you may think when you watch the news, governments do not exist in reality. Sure, the buildings exist, and the people in office exist. But they are just buildings and people. There is no separate entity called government. It is an idea in our heads, and unfortunately a very destructive one because those in government live by the opposite moral code as those outside of government. While it is unethical for you to take money from your neighbor or initiate force without consent, that is the lifeblood of those in government.

If you travel to capitals you will often see grand buildings. Think about how those were created. They are built using money forcefully extracted from the people living in that area. If a free market entrepreneur can afford a large house it is because he enriched other people's lives, but a government building arises because other people's property rights were violated and their wealth was plundered.

According to professor R.J. Rummel, during the 20th century alone, governments around the world were responsible for the deaths of 262 million deaths (Rummel, 2002). Your mind may immediately go to the World Wars and others as the cause, but wars are not included in his numbers. Even without those additions this is about 6 times the amount of people than were killed during the wars of the 20th century. Numbers like this one should at least give people reason to question the system in which they life.

> Just to give perspective on this incredible murder by government, if all these bodies were laid head to toe, with the average height being 5', then they would circle the earth ten times.
>
> R.J. Rummel,
> American political scientist, 2002

I think it is important to distinguish one's affinity for the people, restaurants, marketplace and environment in an area from the government which is living off of the people's backs.

The Secrets to Nonviolent Prosperity

Chapter 6

360° ECONOMICS

For every action we take, there are others which we cannot simultaneously take. For example, if you purchase an iPod, you cannot spend that money on anything else. It is already used up. We put our money toward what we most value.

But when we are taxed, that money can no longer go to where we would have spent it. What does this mean? Since we have less money under our control, we will demand fewer and different products and services.

This dramatically changes the economic landscape, as businesses that would have been thriving if people had all of their money now do not have enough to survive. Demand is artificially shifted toward government agencies, businesses which have government contracts and companies which are somehow benefitting from the legislation and taxation. This chapter is titled 360° Economics because we will be looking at the impact of economic decisions from all different angles.

In the mid-1800's, the French economist Frederic Bastiat introduced the concept of "what is seen and what is not seen," in his book, *The Law*. Whenever people are forced to pay for something, they look at what that money was spent on (what is seen), but rarely do they look at what they *did not* get to spend the money on (what is not seen).

When people are free to spend their money as they choose, the economy will shift to meet those demands. If people are forced to pay for a product, then the economy will shift to meet the demands of the politicians, while the individuals still have needs that they are not able to fulfill because they do not have the money. You may think that the politicians are representatives of the people, but if their choices were the same in the first place, then taxes would not be necessary because people's money would already be going to the same places, minus the bureaucrats' salaries.

One of the greatest fallacies in economics which affects us all is looking only at the immediate consequences of a policy for a specific group, and not the long-term impacts for everyone. Because special interest groups have had great incentive to convince people that certain policies which benefit them should be passed, we are all suffering the long-term consequences of yesterday's policies.

Imagine a company lobbying to get legislation passed which will benefit them to the tune of $300 million. The taxes would come from 10 million residents, so each person would pay an average of $30. The company might be willing to spend up to $270 million to get the legislation passed, while the average effected person will probably pay $30 or less in their efforts to oppose it. If the people paid any higher, they would be paying more to not pay the taxes than the taxes themselves. People can certainly band together on certain issues and defeat special-interest groups, but the odds are stacked against them. The likely outcome is that the $300 million bill will pass, directing people's money away from where they would have spent it and toward where they are forced to spend it.

Let's go back to the local library scenario and follow the path of the money. The total amount to keep the library open was several million dollars. What the people in the community see is the library reopening: kids having stories read to them, students doing research, etc. That is following the path of where the money went, but even more important is looking at where the money did not go. Each person is out about $500, which means that they have $500 less to spend on things they would have chosen, such as food and housing, or increasing their savings for their future. As a result, the proprietors of those establishments which would have been patronized will suffer with decreased sales, with some forced to close. When this decreased spending money is multiplied by hundreds, thousands or millions, the economic effects are tremendous.

The following are examples of this key lesson in action. Hopefully, by the end of this chapter you will be able to read headlines about economic stimulus packages or new city-funded sports coliseums and not just take them at face value. You will be able to look at the situation from all different angles and be able to see the various consequences.

BAILOUTS

THE SCENARIO:
The government steps in to save a specific company or many companies by providing them with a cash infusion or by taking them over. This is a common occurrence when the economy is in a downturn and certain companies or industries are deemed important enough to warrant propping them up. The government claims that these companies are so important that they cannot be allowed to fail. Everyone will benefit from saving the auto, airline or bank company, they say.

THE REAL EFFECTS:

The great thing about the business world in a truly free market, compared to the political one, is that when a business is not running profitably, it will change tactics or go out of business. When a big company is running at a loss and is near bankruptcy, that means people do not value the product as highly as the money they would need to give up for it in exchange. It could be for any number of reasons, but the fact is that people would rather spend their money elsewhere. If a big business is performing poorly and the customers are not satisfied, that is a huge opportunity for an entrepreneur to compete with the failing business.

2008 saw the largest Federal bailout programs ever, which totaled over $8.5 *trillion*! That amount is greater than the expense of all the previous US wars *combined* (Lucas, 2008).

> The ultimate result of shielding men from the effects
> of folly is to fill the world with fools.
>
> Herbert Spencer,
> English philosopher, 1844

WHO IS HELPED:

The propped up businesses certainly benefit from being saved, and the politicians may get some contributions from the companies they helped. When the government takes over banks that are failing, as happened in 2008, it benefits by gaining more control over the banking system.

WHO IS HURT:

The money that is given to the companies comes from taxes. That means the tax-payers are hurt because their property rights were violated and they now have less money to save or spend at their discretion.

The competitors are hurt as well. In a free market, a business is punished when it is not running well by losing its customers and investors and going out of business. But when it is saved, the business is more willing to take risks. This makes it very hard for the competitors who would normally be able to take advantage of being more efficient.

Other industries are hurt as well because people have less disposable income with which to patronize other businesses.

Rather than just looking at the big company that has been saved, think about the vast amount of money that people will not be able to spend on things they value more, and how those companies which would have gotten some of people's money will not be able to flourish because of this. It is a mistake to think that allowing a business to fail would condemn those workers to unemployment. What would occur would be a redirection of employment.

When large companies are getting a bailout, often times the situation is more complex than that they simply are not being run well. For example, the auto and airline businesses have to deal with unions and other restrictive legislation which make their production of cars and planes more expensive than they would be in the free market. It is government intervention in the market which causes these companies to be failing in the first place, and it is more government intervention, in the form of bailouts, which is used to temporarily prop-up the businesses. The solution to the problems created by the government is not more intervention, but rather a removal of the initial problem (the government), thus allowing true free market competition.

MINIMUM-WAGE LAWS

THE SCENARIO:

Minimum-wage is a pay rate set by the government - state and federal - that makes it illegal for an employer to pay the employees less than the stated amount. It is also illegal for someone who is willing to work for below minimum-wage to accept that amount.

THE REAL EFFECTS:

If there were no downside to minimum-wage laws, then they certainly would be wonderful. The minimum could be set at $1 million dollars and everyone would be rich. Unfortunately, the consequences of these laws are just the opposite of what are intended. They end up hurting more people than they are helping. The forced higher wage acts to shrink the supply of labor, and thus lead to unemployment.

WHO IS HELPED:

The employees who are worth more to their employers than the new minimum-wage are helped. For example: if the new minimum is $8/hr and an employee is worth $10/hr to the company, then that person will remain employed and receive the new, higher minimum-wage. Those who are not worth more than the minimum-wage to the company will no longer be employed there.

WHO IS HURT:

All of the people who are not worth the minimum-wage to an employer feel the negative effects of these laws. These include people who were working at a lower rate and people who were not previously working. This law makes it illegal for someone willing to work for less than the minimum-wage to accept that lower amount. The employers will thus hire fewer people, lowering their overall productivity. Without government intervention, particularly minimum-wage laws, the unemployment rate could be nearly zero. Everybody who wanted a job would be able to find one because they would always be able to compete on the amount of money they were willing to receive.

Minimum-wage in particular hurts teens, who are just starting out trying to get some experience, and the elderly. People get paid more when they are more valuable to an employer, and they become more valuable by getting skills and experience. Generally, people need to work their way up, and having a minimum-wage cuts many people off from that opportunity.

Ultimately, when there is a minimum-wage the unemployment rate goes up and the productivity of businesses goes down because they cannot hire as many people. When productivity goes down, or is not allowed to increase as fast as it would in an unhampered market, the value of our money goes down because we cannot buy as many goods with it as we could have. If wages are allowed to go down to their market level, there would be full employment, the supply of goods would dramatically increase, and even though some nominal wages would be lower, the purchasing power would be higher.

I sympathize with people who appreciate increases in the minimum-wage. Most of us want to improve our condition, and getting more money for one's job is a sign of personal improvement. While it is very difficult to live on minimum-wage, it is even harder to get by when you are unemployed, if there is no welfare or unemployment insurance. My intent is not to create ill-will between the minimum-wage employed and the unemployed, but rather to show a way that the lives can improve for each person. Having our monetary system be 100% commodity-based would improve people's conditions to a much greater degree than was even proposed by the minimum-wage law advocates.

When the money supply contracts and we go into a depression, like the Great Depression, prices of goods fall because the demand for the products has decreased. If there are minimum-wage laws and union legislation which legally set the wage rates above what the market rate would be, then you are looking at increasing unemployment. Because wages are not allowed to adjust along with the price of goods, the employers have to lay off employees.

PRICE FIXING

THE SCENARIO:

Price fixing is when the government steps in and makes it illegal to either charge above or below a certain amount. It occurs in many industries where consumers become worried about escalating prices or companies become worried over decreasing prices pinching their bottom line. When a "price ceiling" occurs in the market of apartments, it is called "rent control", which is sold to the masses as a way to make housing more affordable by putting upper limits on rates that can be charged. Cities like New York and San Francisco have rent control in certain areas to make them more accessible to those with less means. A "price floor" is meant to protect the producers and give them more profit by not allowing more efficient competitors to charge lower prices.

> By what conceivable standard can the policy of price-fixing be a crime when practiced by businessmen, but a public benefit when practiced by the government?
>
> Ayn Rand,
> Philosopher and novelist, 1962

THE REAL EFFECTS:
The price of an item is at the meeting point of supply and demand. If the price is fixed below the free market level, a shortage will occur when people realize the item is undervalued as they demand greater quantities. Imagine if all new computers had to be sold at $100. The manufacturers would be sold out within a matter of minutes, and they would never be able to keep up with demand. They would also lose incentive to make improvements to the computers because they would not be getting a fair market price. In this situation where there is a shortage, rationing would likely take place. If the government deems the company or product valuable enough, they will subsidize the costs of production, thus allowing the company to profit while selling at below market levels. This subsidy money has to be taken from other people though, through taxes, causing other industries to contract.

> The 1978 order, which a federal appeals court upheld last year, barred Borden from pricing its ReaLemon reconstituted lemon juice at "unreasonably" low levels.
> *The Wall Street Journal*, 3/2/1983

CASE STUDY: *New York City Rent Control*
Parts of New York City have been under rent control since early in World War II. Since the landlords are not allowed to charge the market value for their properties, their profit margin is greatly reduced or altogether wiped away. The decreased revenue leads to fewer funds available for repairs and improvements. A mutual resentment can grow between the landlord and the tenants because the landlord is not getting the amount that he should be getting (that others would be willing to pay) and the tenants are paying for a place which is falling apart and not being fixed-up. As the cost of maintaining a building keeps going up due to inflation, many

landlords cannot stay in business and choose to abandon their buildings.

You may be wondering where all the people will go who currently live in rent-controlled housing. The effect of rent control is to decrease the supply of housing in that area compared to what it would be in the free market because property owners lose the incentive to create more housing. Since the supply is reduced, those who would have been able to afford the prime locations but could not find an opening, are forced to move to neighboring areas which are not rent controlled. This artificially increases the housing demand in these surrounding areas which results in higher prices. This makes it especially challenging for those with less means.

If there weren't rent control, the supply of housing would increase which would decrease the demand for housing in the neighboring areas, resulting in price decreases. The other main obstacles are zoning laws and building permits. If the development of people's land was not artificially restricted, the amount of housing would likely escalate in these areas, thereby meeting the demands of both those with low and high incomes alike.

The victims of rent control - the landlords and the people who could afford to live in the area but could not find a place - suffer more than the beneficiaries because if rent control laws were repealed, the building industry would make up for lost time, very quickly increasing the supply and quality of apartments. Abandoned buildings would be rebuilt and the competition would actually bring the prices down over time (adjusted for inflation). Those who had lived in rent-controlled housing would certainly be able to find affordable housing after the laws were repealed because the increase in supply in those neighborhoods would decrease the price, and the decreased demand in surrounding areas would lower those prices.

Even though people with more money will continually come into the more desirable areas, making them pricier, that money is leaving other areas, making those less expensive.

WHO IS HELPED:
A price ceiling helps those who are able to get the products at the lower price.

A price floor helps the less efficient producers.

WHO IS HURT:
Both price ceilings and price floors prevent resources from going to where they are most valued. Price floors force people to pay more for an item than they would need to in the free market, and thus they have less money to spend elsewhere. Those other industries that would have gotten money either do not grow as fast or decline correspondingly. If a company cannot survive and make a profit on its own, then it should change approaches or cease business.

What would happen to the recently unemployed? They would go to where they were of more value to an employer.

> After many oppressions which Diocletian put into practice had brought a general shortage upon the empire, he set himself to regulate the prices of all vendible things. There was also much blood shed upon very slight and trifling accounts; and the people brought provisions no more to the markets, since they could not get a reasonable price for them; and this increased the shortages so much, that at last after many had died by it, the law itself was laid down.
>
> Lactantius,
> Roman historian, ca 301 A.D.

Price ceilings do not allow the owner to sell or rent the product at a rate that is mutually agreeable. It is not the case that the price would be raised so high that no one could afford it - that would be irrational. The business owners would try to maximize the return they get for their product, and likewise the consumers would try to maximize what they would be getting for the price. An agreement will only be reached in the free market if each party believes they are getting something of greater value than they are giving up.

As noted earlier, price ceilings lead to product shortages. In rent-controlled housing, this prevents neighborhoods from improving because landlords lose their incentive to keep up and improve their properties. All of the businesses that would have catered to improving the residences are hurt by price ceilings.

> Whereas...it hath been found by experience that limitations upon the prices of commodities are not only ineffectual for the purposes proposed, but likewise productive of very evil consequences to the great detriment of the public service and grievous oppression of individuals...resolved that it be recommended to the several states to repeal or suspend all laws or resolutions within the said states respectively limiting, regulating or restraining the Price of any Article, Manufacture or Commodity.
> Continental Congress, 1778

TARIFFS

THE SCENARIO:
Tariffs are taxes on imports which raise the prices people pay for those goods domestically. There are two purposes of the tariff: the

first is to raise taxes, thereby increasing government revenue, and the second is to protect domestic production.

THE REAL EFFECTS:

When tariffs are applied, people are not able to get the products as inexpensively as they would be able to in a completely free market. What does this mean for the resources? They will not go to where they are most valued. Tariffs interfere with people's ability to utilize their competitive advantage because they are not able to give the consumer as good a deal as on the free market.

> No undertaking is more futile than that of trying to base the prosperity of the parts on the ruination of the whole. And yet this is what the policy of protectionism seeks to do.
>
> Frederic Bastiat,
> French economist, 1844

CASE STUDY: *The Light Truck Tariff*

After a year of failed negotiations, the United States turned to retaliatory tariffs in response to the European Economic Community's 1962 decision to raise tariffs on imported chickens, which had served to shut out American producers from the European market. Hoping to hit the European exporters where it hurt, the U.S. government increased tariffs on potato starch, dextrin, brandy and light trucks. While the other tariffs were relaxed over the years, the one on light trucks has remained at 25%, effectively destroying European truck imports.

The domestic truck producers are very supportive of this tariff because it gives them a much bigger profit margin. For example, a foreign truck that the manufacturer would have been willing to sell for $20,000 will have to be sold for at least $25,000 in the U.S.

because of the 25% tariff. Meanwhile, a domestic manufacturer can produce a comparable truck, sell it for $25,000, and keep the $5,000 extra profit that the foreign companies had taxed away. Tariffs tend to protect the less efficient or cause the protected to become less efficient.

For awhile, Japanese manufacturers were able to get around this by exporting the chassis (the truck minus the bed) which was subject to a 4% tariff. Upon arrival in the U.S., a bed was attached, and it was sold as a truck. However, in 1980, the U.S. Customs Service closed this "loophole" due to lobbying by the Big Three auto manufacturers and the United Autoworkers. This domestic protectionism has led many foreign truck manufacturers to construct plants in the U.S. in order to avoid the tariffs. The light truck tariff has virtually shut down non-NAFTA country truck imports, giving a big advantage to domestic producers.

WHO IS HELPED:
The protected domestic companies benefit greatly when their international competitors are forced to pay a tax in order to sell products in that market. And, of course, those who receive the tax money also benefit.

WHO IS HURT:
The foreign producers who are more efficient suffer from this tax because without it they would be able to offer their products at lower prices therefore satisfying more people's needs and making more profit.

The domestic consumers are hurt by this as well because they are being forced to pay more for the products than the prices at which the foreign companies are willing to sell them. This extra money cannot be saved, invested or spent patronizing other industries.

Consumers are also hurt because labor is not being used as efficiently as it could be. If the tariffs did not exist, then a number of domestic businesses, which are currently protected, would not survive. Those employees could be better utilized in other industries which do have competitive advantages. And when resources are used inefficiently, productivity goes down and when there are fewer goods and services to purchase with our money, our purchasing power decreases.

MACHINERY / TECHNOLOGY / INNOVATION

THE SCENARIO:

When new technology is introduced to society to make life easier or businesses run more efficiently, many people fear for their jobs and lobby to halt the new technologies. The claim is that many people will lose their jobs with the new "labor saving" innovation, and that in order to preserve a sound economy with high employment rates, the new technology cannot be allowed.

> Among the most visible of all economic delusions is the belief that machines on net balance create unemployment. Destroyed a thousand times, it has risen a thousand times out of its own ashes as hardy and vigorous as ever.
>
> Henry Hazlitt,
> American economist, 1962

THE REAL EFFECTS:

The fear of losing one's job in the face of "labor-saving" technology is real and justified. But for the most part, the unemployment that results is only temporary. The more efficient new technologies allow more products to reach the market and thus require more people to produce them. What happens is not just a taking over of part of an industry, but rather a growing of the industry. If the people who lost their jobs are able to learn some new skills, then they will be valuable in the growing portion of the industry. Each person who has a new job will become more valuable than they were before.

In 1768, Richard Arkwright invented a cotton-spinning frame when there were estimated to be about 7,900 people working in the production of cotton textiles in England. A parliamentary inquiry twenty-one years later found that number to have risen to 320,000, a 4,400% increase. (Hazlitt, 1996)

In 1910, there were approximately 140,000 employed in the burgeoning American auto industry. As production became better and more efficient and costs decreased, that number went up to 941,000 by 1973.

The purpose of technology in the work environment is to improve production so that more can get done each hour. These innovations lead to reduced costs, which translate to increased production, sales and jobs.

Imagine instead of technology that was making us more productive, it was how long we were working. Would our standard of living be improved if we weren't allowed to work more than five hours per week? That would certainly make people less productive. The result would be very high hourly wage rates (oh yeah!), but also vastly fewer goods produced (oh no!), so the purchasing power of your money would go down roughly in proportion to how little people were allowed to work.

What would happen if instead of work hours being limited, people chose to work longer hours, and work harder? Increased production of goods would cause the prices to drop, thereby increasing the purchasing power of their money, and there would be more capital which could create more jobs as well as better paying ones. The benefits of longer work hours do not need to occur by working more or harder, because we can leverage our productive efforts using labor-saving technology. Those whom did not want to work more than five hours per week would see their wage rates go down, while the harder workers would see theirs go up. Everyone would benefit, though, from the dropping prices due to the general increase in productivity.

Let's look at an island scenario to help illustrate the point. If there were only one person on an island, that person would benefit from working harder and longer. Would anyone be hurt if there were 50,000 completely self-sufficient people on the island and they all decided to work harder and longer? As long as they are respecting property rights, no one is effected by anyone else's productivity because they are all self-sufficient. But as we transition to a division of labor society, everyone's standard of living rises because people are specializing in productive activities such as catching fish, gathering vegetables, making clothes, constructing houses, building sewers and running water systems and many other enterprises valued by the inhabitants. When people work harder and longer hours or introduce technology which increases productivity, these also act to improve the general population's standard of living.

During the time the United States was founded, around 95% of Americans were farmers, many barely supporting themselves. Since then, as better farming methods have been adopted and new machinery has been implemented, that number has dropped to below 5%. 10 times as many people are employed today and our standard of living is vastly greater than they experienced.

I am sure you could imagine spending 10 times the amount of money as you do now, if only you could earn it. Collectively, producing that volume of goods and services in the current state of technology would require 10 times the amount of labor than we are now capable of performing. So rather than an increase in the efficiency of labor causing unemployment, it would enable the the average person to purchase more basic things, such as food and water, and bring former luxury items to the masses, such as cars, computers, and cell phones.

The material progress of humanity is due to being more efficient at getting things done. If it were true that labor-saving technologies caused net unemployment, then by now we should be at about 99.99% unemployment rate. The fact that we are not, and the fact we could have full employment if there were no restrictive labor laws, shows that increasing productive capabilities leads to a raised standard of living, not poverty and unemployment.

WHO IS HELPED:
The only people who are helped are the owners of the protected businesses because they can continue making profit off their outmoded technologies and production methods. Not even the employees benefit in the long run. They will be able to get better paying jobs in the industry where they will be of greater value.

WHO IS HURT:
Pretty much everybody else. The new innovation allows more people to get a better product for a cheaper price. When labor is allowed to flow to industries where they are more valued, then we are able to get more products that we value, thus leading to increased material prosperity. The burgeoning industries create more, better jobs than were taken away. Finding ever more valuable uses for resources is a key to a growing economy, so when

the new technologies are not allowed to come to the market, our economic development is stifled.

TAX-FUNDED PROJECTS AND JOBS

THE SCENARIO:
Got a slow economy? Government spending will save the day. Public works programs are often touted as a way to help out an ailing economy because they give people jobs and undertake projects for society, such as airports, roads, dikes, railroads, and subway systems.

THE REAL EFFECTS:
These jobs and projects are funded by taxes, which means that people now have that much less money to spend, save, or invest. The economy will thus shift away from what the people want and toward what the politicians want, often due to lobbying by corporations and non-profit organizations. Business owners will not be able to hire as many employees because they do not have as much money and consumers will not be able to purchase as many products.

> When government spends, the economy drinks its
> own blood and, in the end, is weakened accordingly.
> Susan Love Brown et al., American political
> anthropologist, 1974

In 2002, three professors in Denmark published their in-depth study of 258 publicly-funded transportation infrastructure projects worth approximately US$90 billion (Flyvbjerg et al., 2002). Allegedly these projects are undertaken with tax support because the private sector would not be willing to risk big losses, and so they will not take on large endeavors. And since the government doesn't have to worry about the profit motive, they can complete the projects at lower costs. The study looked at why costs almost always escalated above the estimate.

They found that the costs of 90% of the projects were underestimated, and that the average actual cost among all types of projects (rail, tunnel, bridges, etc) was 28% higher than estimated. It was found to be a global phenomenon with public works, particularly in the developing world. Looking back over the past 70 years, they found that cost estimating has not become any more accurate. They conclude that the systematic cost underestimation cannot be accounted for by error, but see the only viable explanation being that those who are pushing the projects are purposefully lying to the public about the costs in order to get them going.

While their study does not compare public versus private programs, it is clear that politicians are willing to take this "risk" because they do not have to bear the consequences. Businesses tend to make decisions which most benefit people because those choices also benefit the company, while the government can afford cost escalations because the tax-payers get saddled with the bill. All of the money which gets sapped out of the people's wallets to pay for these high-priced programs diverts money from where it would have gone, which is patronizing other businesses, starting new companies, hiring more employees, and increasing production.

WHO IS HELPED:
People like a guaranteed job, and those with the newly created ones will appreciate them. Remember from earlier that the reason unemployment exists is because of government intervention. If the regulation were not occurring in first place, people would be far less concerned about job security.

WHO IS HURT:

This pattern repeats with each example, so hopefully you are starting to be able to look at the far reaching consequences of such policies. In this case, those private businesses will have decreased productivity as money is drained from the private sector and into the government, leading to lower profits. Consumers will have less money to save or spend, which means they will not be able to provide as well for themselves in the present or the future. Overall productivity will decrease because resources are not going to where people most valued them, and thus with fewer goods and services to purchase, the value of the dollar drops compared to what it would have been in the free market.

UNIONS

THE SCENARIO:

Unions are formed so that employees can speak to the employers with a collective voice. Unions are hailed for raising wages and decreasing work hours. They are unified in fighting the greedy executives to improve the working conditions and increase the wages for the employees. Sounds good.

THE REAL EFFECTS:

Unions do not simply use the power of persuasion to get what they want. If they did, there would be no ethical objection. The problem is that their methods often involve force, whether lobbying for certain laws which protect them or physically beating up those who try to cross the picket line. The effects of these uses of force are extensive.

In 1938, the Fair Labor Standards Act was passed, which established a national minimum-wage, fixed a maximum work week at 40 hours, set a 50% pay increase for overtime work, prohibited people under 16 years old from working in most jobs, and authorized the Department of Labor to enforce the law.

Other pro-union legislation was passed during the New Deal, such as the Norris-LaGuardia Act, which prohibited court injunctions against union violence, and the Wagner Act, which compelled employers to bargain with the unions.

President Hoover used government power to keep union wages artificially high after the Crash of 1929, causing high unemployment rates, and prolonging the Depression.

There is a misconception that unions raise general wage levels, but this can never be true. They certainly can raise wages for those in the union, but only at the cost of lower wages and unemployment for many others. The general level of real wages (purchasing power) increases when productivity increases. Remember from the *quantity theory of money* that general prices can only go up due to a decrease in supply of the goods or an increase in the supply of money. Unions decrease overall productivity and increase wages for those in the unions.

Unions have the force of government on their side when they are dealing with their employers. They can use that force to exclude competing workers, compel unwilling members to join the strike, and make non-members pay for union representation they do not want, while the employers are forced to negotiate with and make concessions to the unions because they are not allowed to fire those who are striking and hire new workers. The strikers are either subsidized by our tax dollars or sometimes by the employer. The unions don't want to use direct violence, and that is why they try to pass legislation which forces the employer to comply with their wishes. But sometimes they see violence as the best means to the end they desire, namely higher wages.

Between 1975 and 1998, the National Institute for Labor Relations Research collected 8,799 incidents of union violence, most of which are against non-union workers, and sometimes against company property. Of these incidents, there were 1,963 arrests and only 258 convictions (Kendrick, 1998). The U.S. Supreme Court's 1973 *Enmons* decision held that union officials may resort to vandalism, assault and even murder so long as the violence was used to secure "legitimate union objectives", such as wage increases. Former Attorney General Edwin Meese testified at a 1997 hearing, that since the *Enmons* decision unions have benefitted from an exemption that "permits union officials - alone among corporate or associational officers in the United States - to use violence and threats of violence to life and property to achieve their goals." (*The Wall Street Journal*, 1997)

WHO IS HELPED:
Those in unions are obviously the group protected by unions. They enjoy greater job security, increased pay and fewer work-hours than their non-union counterparts.

WHO IS HURT:
Once again, nearly everybody else loses. Why? Because unions decrease efficiency. When they force higher pay, fewer people can be hired. When they force fewer work hours at the same cost, less gets done. When they force spread-the-work programs, where there is minute subdivision of labor, time and labor are wasted. In a society where there are a vast number of unions, the members may get higher salaries, but each dollar does not go as far as it would in a truly free market because productivity is greatly decreased. The

idea is not to see how high the numbers in our bank account can go, but rather how much can be purchased for each dollar.

The main problem with unions which use any kind of force - which is nearly all of them - is that they deprive the property owner of their right to do with their property whatever they choose. If an employee does not like the conditions or pay where he works, then that individual is free to look for work elsewhere. But it is not ethical to initiate force against the owner.

When an owner's property rights are not respected, and instead the workers' desires are forcibly attained, then the owner has lost much of the power over his property.

WELFARE AND SOCIAL SECURITY PROGRAMS

THE SCENARIO:
Both of these categories of government programs are easy to sell to the public because they are about helping the disadvantaged. Welfare and Social Security are designed to give aide to the poor and retired, respectively. These programs are thought of as necessary by many people because they believe that government is a benevolent organization, there to take care of our needs.

> In general, the art of government consists of taking as much money as possible from one class of citizens and giving it to another.
>
> Voltaire,
> French philosopher, 1694-1778

THE REAL EFFECTS:
Both of these programs are paid for through taxes, with Social Security in particular taking a large chunk. A lot of money is involuntarily redistributed from going to where it is most valued to where it is less valued.

Social Security

In 1935, the Social Security Act was passed as part of the New Deal, less than a year after Italian immigrant Charles Ponzi, was released from prison after 10 years and deported to Italy. What do these two things have to do with one another? Everything.

Mr. Ponzi was able to convince a dozen or so people that they would be able to reap a 50% profit in 45 days by trading international postal coupons through him, starting in December of 1919. Mr. Ponzi kept his word when the first 45 day time period came to a close, and paid the "investors" $375 for the $250 they initially gave to him. Excited by the quick turnaround of profit, most people chose to "reinvest" their money with him. News of this great money-making system spread quickly as a way of making everyone rich. By April, 1920, he was taking in $250,000 per day, and within 6 months he had collected over $10 million. His name was known throughout the country, he bought a large estate and spent money lavishly.

His financial success came crashing down very soon after though, when his system was figured out, thanks to a tip that he was a former criminal. His money making system was very simple: he would take the money from the second round of people to pay for the first, take from the third round to pay for the second, take from the fourth round to pay for the third, and so on. As you can see, not everyone can win in the long run. The early "investors" had to reap their profits in order for them and others to believe in the system. Then it was just a matter of getting more and more money coming in, until he decided to run with the money. Every group of "investors" will necessarily need to be bigger than the previous group so that the previous group can get the profits they expect. Eventually the system would have to collapse, with the last, and biggest round of "investors" left high and dry.

Social Security is the same scam Charles Ponzi duped the American people with 90 years ago, but much more harmful and unethical. People are forced to participate in Social Security, it is vastly larger and people can not only financially ruin themselves but their children's generation as well. Just like the Ponzi scheme, there were some early winners in Social Security who got out more than they put in, but the burden on some to support the others gets greater and greater, until it necessarily collapses. Already the number of workers needed to support one person receiving Social Security benefits has dropped from 16 in 1950 down to a little over 3 today. To make this more clear, let's say that one person on Social Security is receiving $1000 per month. If that money comes from 16 people, then on average each person contributes $62.50. However, when there are only 3 people to cover the thousand dollars, the average contribution is $333.33. This is over a 500% increase in the burden on each person who is contributing to Social Security.

Most people think that Social Security is like a trust fund where the money you pay in while you work is put into an account for you for when you retire. The truth is that the money you pay in goes directly out to support those on Social Security. The government purposefully misrepresents Social Security. It has to in order to get people's support since it is based on fraud.

This Act came about during the New Deal, when politicians were becoming more empowered to promise the public that they could eliminate unemployment, raise wages, increase the standard of living, reduce rents and interest rates, etc. Unfortunately, the result of government programs which have these aims is actually to decrease the standard of living because government does not produce anything that it does not already take away from others.

> When the people are weak the state is strong; when the state is weak the people are strong. Hence the state that follows a true course strives to weaken the people... In a state where the virtuous are treated as if they were depraved, order shall reign and the state surely shall be powerful.
>
> Shang Yang,
> Chinese statesman, 4th century B.C.

WHO IS HELPED:
Welfare recipients gain short run benefits. Social Security recipients do not have short run benefits, and the money they gain in the long run will often be less than the amount they put in when inflation and opportunity costs are factored in.

WHO IS HURT:
Let's first address the psychological effect that these programs have on people. They both decrease one's incentive to take personal responsibility and be productive. Those who are most productive (receiving the most money for their work) are punished the most in the form of higher taxes, in order to support the least productive. When someone can choose between getting approximately the same amount for either working or not, the choice to not work is obvious to many. I will use exaggerated benefits to illustrate how this works. Imagine that welfare recipients received $1 million per year. Do you think more or fewer people would try to get on Welfare? One would have to make significantly more than $1 million to not want to go on Welfare. The principle is the same

when the benefit is approximately what one can make on a minimum-wage job.

The same goes for Social Security. But in this case, rather than taking care of one's self in the present, it is about caring for one's future financial needs. This entitlement system leads people to take less responsibility for their finances. If we were not guaranteed money in later life, then we would tend to be wiser about how we spent, saved and invested. This is true no matter what one's level of income.

The other side of the entitlement programs are the tax-payers. As more people get older, there are fewer young people to provide the money for each person living on Social Security. This means that each working person will have a larger portion of their income going to support the retired. This is very debilitating for the individual and the economy as a whole. When people are not allowed to save and spend as they choose, the whole economy shifts away from what people really want toward what the politicians want.

There are voluntary ways to assist people who are struggling in their lives. The problem is when the coercion of government is involved. People are generally less willing to give voluntarily to those in need when a large portion of their pay is already being taken away for similar purposes.

These programs did not fill a void when they were introduced, but rather pushed aside and made less significant the thousands of private charities and mutual aid organizations that already existed.

Fraternal societies, such as the Elks, Odd Fellows and the Knights of Pythias, were very popular until the middle of the 20th century, when the government intervention pushed them out. These organizations were rivaled only by churches as institutional providers of social services. The poor, and a myriad of racial and ethnic minorities, particularly took advantage of the fellowships as a way to insure they could be taken care of in times when they were sick or old, without having to rely on charity. These organizations helped to facilitate community as well as strong character. In 1944, Swedish economist Gunnar Myrdal asserted in a study that there were over 4,000 associations in Chicago formed by the city's 275,000 black residents (Boaz, 1997).

When government intervention ceases, businesses will grow, mutual aid associations will sprout up and charitable giving will rise. In my experience most people are caring and want to help one another out. The key is whether the assistance comes from voluntary or coercive action.

Chapter 7

MYTHS THAT PERSIST

A myth is a widely held but false belief, like the Greek mythology that is studied in school. While it can be interesting to learn about the beliefs of ancient cultures it can be quite powerful to see through the myths of our own time. When certain beliefs are commonly held, it can be hard to look critically at them and find out the truth. People are free to have their beliefs, but many try to force their ways on others in the form of legislation.

Many people hold onto certain economic beliefs not because they make sense on thorough inspection, but because they were led to believe they were true and they strike an emotional chord. The following are some economic myths that persist, despite being refuted by reason and evidence. These myths have a tremendous impact on how we live our lives and the state of our economy. Let's take a look at some notable ones.

MYTH: A NATION SHOULD BE SELF-SUFFICIENT

This rhetoric is often used to ignite the flames of patriotism. Appealing to people only to purchase domestically manufactured products, and cut off our dependence on foreign oil can be an effective way to create superficial solidarity among a group of people. But in terms of its economic impact domestically, it would be devastating to withdraw from international trade, even if it was only for those things which people think are most fundamental, such as energy.

Why is this?

The principles of trade are the same whether two people, a town, a country or the whole planet is involved. This desire for self-sufficiency undermines the division of labor and competitive advantages, and leads a lot of people to engage in the same work, less efficiently.

Let's start with each person desiring to be self-sufficient. The individual wants to feel secure and in charge of his own life, so he decides to grow and make his own food, some clothes, and even build a dwelling. Granted, none of it is high quality, but he is self-sufficient, and he is surviving. Imagine if everyone had this desire. There would be no businesses because people would not trade. Everyone would be doing the same work, inefficiently, and hopefully surviving (though this sort of society could not support a number of people anywhere close to our current population).

How do we get to prosperity? By specializing, utilizing competitive advantages and economies of scale, where as production increases, the cost per unit produced decreases. Someone with particular knowledge or skills can specialize and develop a business to trade their products and services with others. Those others are also specializing and growing their businesses. Every working person has got some sort of competitive advantage, whether they are skill sets, location or willingness to work cheaply. When people are allowed to utilize these advantages, resources go to where they are most valued.

If Americans are able to get cheaper labor for certain products overseas, the people who no longer have those jobs domestically can use their skills in more valued ways. In the free market, every resource tends to go to where it is most valued. If you are overqualified, your job will likely be done by someone who is a better match, and you can move to a job where you can maximize your value. Many companies take advantage of labor abroad which is less expensive because there are fewer of the labor and business regulations, which drive up the costs of doing business in the United States.

If Americans tried to produce all of their energy domestically, a tremendous amount of workers would go into that protected industry, evacuating many others. Yes, we could produce all of our energy requirements domestically, but at a sacrifice to other parts of the economy. We would be paying artificially high prices for the products. That extra money spent and those jobs taken could not be used in other industries where they were more valued in the free market. If we had a truly free market and oil still cost more to extract domestically than abroad, but Americans wanted domestically produced oil anyways, then we would be paying a premium unnecessarily. On the other hand, if oil production turned out to be cheaper domestically once there was a free market, then it would make economic sense for Americans as well as foreigners to patronize the American oil production.

Vast oil reserves in the U.S. have been blocked from being productive. This government intervention lowers the supply of energy that would be available domestically, resulting in higher prices, and our searching abroad for cheaper sources.

Don't we need to be energy independent as a backup plan in case something happens to our source country? The same thing could be said by regions of the country, states and even cities. What if all of our energy is produced domestically, and a natural disaster strikes the processing facilities? This is the wonderful thing about free trade: we can get energy from many sources around the world, and if one goes offline, others will fill that space. If we were allowed to use our own resources, certainly those would contribute to the overall energy supply domestically. But my idea of a good backup plan is not having all of one's eggs in one basket. If foreign energy becomes more expensive than it would cost to produce our own, then domestic energy companies will sprout up in the free market.

MYTH: LOCAL IS BETTER

An extension of the self-sufficiency myth, the belief that locally produced and sold goods and services are better is fueling a massive trend in all sorts of consumer goods. What are the aspects of this view? When something is produced and sold locally, jobs and money stay in the community. It is also believed that resources are used more efficiently when the economy is local because transportation costs and environmental externalities are decreased, such as CO_2 emissions from planes, trains, trucks and ships.

When a community of people prefer not to trade on a larger scale, and instead want things produced locally, they have to go to jobs where they are less valued. These communities are not able to take advantage of economics of scale and thus prices for products go up. While people may take home the same amount of money, the higher costs of goods makes their money not go as far, leaving them with less money to invest in growing businesses. The cutting edge jobs are abandoned because people need to take care of their more basic needs. An isolated economy will very quickly become impoverished. This is why most people who promote the "local is better" ideology don't extend their beliefs to cars, electronics, and really anything that is complex. They'll say things like, "well those can come from abroad but local is better for the simple and essential items, such as food."

But this is not logical. The argument for each town growing their own produce is the same as each making their own cars. If that is your specialty, and you have a competitive advantage, then go for it, otherwise you are wasting resources: time, energy, money and raw materials. Trade on a large scale does take certain jobs away from locals - the jobs that could be done more efficiently elsewhere. The locals whose jobs were taken by more efficient competitors can find new jobs where their skills are more highly valued. This way money and jobs still stay local, and shipping costs are relatively low because of economies of scale. The locals will get better products, and the services they provide will be more highly valued. Its a win-win.

The argument against the need for a local backup plan - meaning local production of food - is that same as the one against energy independence. The best backup plan is being diverse in the sources of our goods. If all of the food was produced locally, and a natural disaster wiped out the supply, there goes the backup plan. But if the world is open to you, and you had a natural disaster, and so did ten of your sources, you would still have many possible businesses with which to trade.

The local food production argument also ignores the masses of people who live in cities or other areas which are not conducive to growing food. Can you imagine if New York City had to grow all of its own food, let alone produce all of the other products it uses? I can't either. There are certain locations where the land and climate are particularly good for growing food. The locals can take advantage of this by purchasing their food locally. However, many places are not good for growing food, and the people in those places will import the food from the locales which are good for food production. This makes the food less expensive for locals as well as those consumers who are further away.

Many are concerned that patronizing chain companies rather than local establishments leads to money being sucked out of the community and going to the company headquarters, thereby destroying local businesses. You can look at this situation in several ways: that the chains are destroying the local companies by offering either better products or lower prices, or maybe even both; that the consumers are destroying the local businesses by choosing to purchase the better and cheaper goods; or that the local companies are destroying themselves by not offering products and services that are as good or better than the competition at prices more attractive to the consumers. Money is flowing to these companies because people are making the free choice of what to do with it.

Nothing is stopping people locally from creating a successful business that people elsewhere will appreciate, thereby sucking money away from those consumers and into your community. The belief that things should be produced and purchased locally really cannot even work in a society where people want to improve their condition. Just think about where your car was manufactured, and where the parts came from. Think about where the tools and machinery needed for agriculture are made, and how those factories were made, and where and how those materials were originally mined. Think about where your clothes were manufactured, where the materials were created, where the dyes came from, and how all of the machinery which created these elements was manufactured. Take anything you own or see and think about everything that was needed to bring it into existence - the resources, the labor and the ingenuity. As you peel back the layers of production, it becomes evident that it takes much of the world to bring together the products we use, from the simplest to the most complex.

To me this is a fascinating thought process which humbles me every time. I am amazed by the interconnectivity of it all. If our preference was strictly for locally produced goods then we would be living a very primitive lifestyle indeed.

MYTH: FREE MARKETS INCREASE INEQUALITY

> The forces of a capitalist society, if left unchecked, tend to make the rich richer and the poor poorer.
> Jawaharlal Nehru,
> Prime Minister of India, 1958

The rich get richer, and the poor get poorer. That is the persistent belief about the results of the free market.

It is obvious looking at the wealthiest people in the world over the past two decades that the rich have indeed gotten richer. But this is not a bad thing. When someone gets wealthy, many people benefit by being able to purchase products or services for lower prices, thus having their dollar go further. In the genuinely free market, the rich do indeed get richer, and so do the poor.

The wealthy people raise the standard of living for everyone. The poor in America today live with conveniences and modern amenities the upper class lived without just a century ago. The people in extreme poverty in the world are not poor because others are rich, but because their property rights are not respected.

In these difficult times we are facing now, the idea that the general standard of living has increased for the majority of people in the world over the past century may not seem so obvious. This does not mean that the condition has improved for those in the most destitute of circumstances. In fact, there is a long way to go. I am saddened by the conditions of poverty that many people are in around the world, as well as the way people's hard earned money is being stripped away from them during this economic collapse. This is one of the main reasons I am writing this book. *The fastest track there is to having people's needs and desires met is for property rights to be understood and respected.*

In a truly free market, monetary inequality originates from a difference in creativity and ambition, which makes possible different levels of wealth accumulation, and thereby inheritance. Those people who do not have either will not be as wealthy as those who do, but their standard of living will still rise because they will be able to purchase the mass produced products that the creative and ambitious are making.

> We cannot equalize wealth without equalizing people. There is no way to equalize people except by killing them. Men have equal skills only in the grave.
>
> Gary North,
> American writer, 1982

Most poor people are not poor because they lack resources, as so many have been led to believe. This belief leads many politicians to appease public opinion by giving foreign aid to struggling countries. While these monies are gifts to the foreign governments, they are thefts from domestic individuals. When we have money taken away from us against our wishes, we have less money to spend, to save and to invest as we choose, thus slowing down our economy.

John Stossel, of ABC News, reported that the people living in Kenyan slums were not wanting foreign aid, they were wanting security of their property rights. In these slums, there are a number of small businesses, but since the people do not actually own the land, their incentive to expand is greatly diminished. It follows that if they do not own the land, their businesses are not secure from arbitrary government decisions, including demolition. He reported that over the past 50 years western governments have given African governments over half of a *trillion* dollars, but many African nations are even poorer now than they were before. The money and goods that are given to these governments have a way of getting "lost" while on their way to the poor (Stossel).

If foreign aid was abandoned and property rights were respected, I am certain that investments would pour into these regions. Foreign aid is not the answer because money is not the problem. The people's goods are not secure, so the corrupt governments can take their property and close their businesses arbitrarily. If one's property is not secure, there is a disincentive to expand one's business.

When International Monetary Fund loans are given to the governments of Third World countries, the people of those countries become indebted to both the government and the IMF. Many of these loans simply cannot be paid off, so land and natural resources are sometimes taken instead of payment. Remember that the nature of fractional-reserve loans is that it is mathematically impossible for all of them to be paid off, the result being that these countries become debt-ridden, and economically weak.

If there are just and stable laws based on property rights and the non-aggression principle, then the economy will start to grow. Wealthier individuals can then make intelligent investments in some of these growing businesses.

RACE AND THE FREE MARKET

Most people believe that the United States is a capitalist country, and when that view is combined with people's awareness of the facts that while black people make up 13.4% of the population, they are 39.8% of welfare recipients, their prison density in relation to their population is about 6 times that of whites, and they receive a disproportionately small amount of the personal income, many come to the conclusion that capitalism is the cause of the inequality. As a result of this, capitalism is condemned as the system which exploits black people.

However, this conclusion does not follow. Far from being the source of such injustices, capitalism is the solution for them. The system we have today in the United States is not even semi-capitalism; it is more regulated than free. Wherever there is a government there cannot be a truly free market, and as the size of government grows, the market will become further regulated and restricted.

Capitalism is an economic system based on individual property rights, in which each individual is free to act peaceably to achieve his or her own gain. It is a system in which businesspeople are free to do that which they consider to be most profitable to themselves. Workers are free to seek the highest wages they can find, and consumers are free to seek the lowest prices they can find. The sole restriction is that no one can resort to the initiation of force. It is under a system of capitalism that each businessperson, worker and consumer are free from the legally condoned initiation of force.

This means that all ethical actions would be nonviolent, and the law would be against those who initiated violence.

Race and Wages
The following will illustrate the point that in a genuine free market economy, even very small wage differences could not be maintained. Assume that white workers of a certain skill get $10/hr, while black workers of the same skill can be hired at just 5% less, or $9.50. A factory must employ 500 laborers of this skill level, so with a 40-hr week, over a 50-week year, this slight difference in wage rates results in a savings to the company of $500,000 [(10 x 500 x 40 x 50) - (9.50 x 500 x 40 x 50) = 500,000]. This is $500,000 of extra profit to the company just for hiring 500 black instead of white people.

The same is true of a small business where only 10 employees are hired. It would still be more profitable to hire black employees, which would result in an extra profit of $10,000 [0.50 x 10 x 40 x 50 = 10,0000].

It is doubtful whether there are many employers which are so prejudiced as to throw away $500,000 per year in the case of the larger firm, or even of $10,000 in the case of the smaller one, just to indulge their personal preference for white people.

Let's think about the implications: most businesspeople would not be able to resist hiring black over white people due to this small wage difference. Every difference in wages that was based on the color of one's skin, no matter how big or small, would result in increased demand for black labor and decreased for white. This increased demand would lead to higher wages for black people and lower for the whites, until they met at an equilibrium.

Racist employers, in the truly free market, will lose out to those employers which are solely concerned with maximizing profit. If an employer has a choice between two equally good workers, the one who is willing to work for less will be hired. If the choice is between two people at the same price, the employer will choose the better worker. If the employer disregards skill and cost in order to hire a racial preference, that will result in extra business costs and less profit.

Let's say that initially most employers in a given area are so prejudiced that they are willing to forego the extra profit. The result would be that the minority of business owners who hired black employees at the lower cost would be able to earn this extra profit. This would increase the income of the minority of owners, allowing them to save more and invest in further business expansion, all the while taking business away from the bigoted majority of owners.

The result in this free market example would be that employers who did not hire based on skin-color would tend to replace prejudiced ones. In this way, capitalism acts to ensure that race is not a factor in the workforce, because even those businesspeople who choose to put race above all else will see their sales dramatically shrink over time. The results will be a transformation of the culture from prejudiced to practical.

If the free market were allowed to equalize the wage rates for black and white workers, assuming the skills were the same, the result would be a substantially greater increase in income for the black employees than the decrease for the white ones. Let's assume that there are approximately 5 white people to each black person in the population, and that the income of the black person is about half that of the white, at \$10/hr compared to \$20/hr. If we take the cumulative income of 6 people per hour (5 whites and 1 black), it comes to $110 [(20 x 5) + (1 x 10) = 110]. The average wage then, is $18.33/hr [110/6 = 18.33]. So if the free market is allowed to equalize the wages, the drop in the wages for white people would be about 8.35% [(20-18.33)/20 = 8.35%], while the increase in wages for black people would be 83.3% [(18.33-10)/10 = 83.3%].

It is important to note that this decrease in nominal wages for white workers would not result in a lower living standard. Since the supply of workers has increased, production costs have gone down, thereby reducing the costs of goods. So even this nominal wage reduction is actually a real wage increase, meaning each dollar has more purchasing power than before.

Minorities and Housing

Minorities would be supplied with goods on the same terms as white people in the genuinely free market. To see how this works, let's first assume that this is not the case. Let's say that the rents minorities pay are 5% higher than white tenants pay, while the costs to the landlords are the same. If a landlord's profit rate was normally 10%, the 5% additionally received from minorities would constitute a 50% increase in profits [5% / 10% = 50%]. This high level of profit would lead to an increase in housing for minorities. This increase in supply would result in a decrease in the prices paid, resulting in an equilibrium with what white tenants pay. Thus, in the free market, minorities would not pay anymore for rents compared to white people.

The government that we live under has rent-control in some locations, which is largely responsible for the deterioration and the abandonment of buildings in the ghettos in which it exists. Rent-control has worse effects on black people because of their poverty. This is due to the fact that they tend to live where the land values are lower than other areas. Rent-control prices are already close to operating costs as opposed to rent covering costs and profit. As the

191

money supply increases (inflation), operating costs go up, including property taxes, and under rent-control, landlords are compelled to absorb these increases. This results in less money for the landlord with which to do maintenance, and when operating costs exceed rent, and there is no relief in the foreseeable future, the landlord will often just abandon the building. It is the landlords in the poorer neighborhoods who first abandon their buildings because their costs are already close to the rent. So black people are often the first to suffer the negative consequences of rent-control.

Because there is no profit incentive in public housing, it tends to quickly deteriorate into slums. While a private apartment owner is motivated to keep the investment as valuable as possible because it is his own money invested, government officials have no such motivation. It does not make any personal financial difference to the government bureaucrat what kind of tenants moved in, or what they do, to the public housing.

Race and Urban Merchants

It is often noted that merchants in minority neighborhoods charge higher prices for goods than in suburban, predominantly white neighborhoods. The above example applies to this situation as well. The higher prices charged for goods in more dangerous neighborhoods do not constitute price gouging, but rather a higher cost of business. In fact, often times the higher prices still are not high enough to cover the costs, and the result is businesses moving away from the violent neighborhoods and not towards them, depriving people living in these areas of places to shop.

Let's say that a grocery store usually has a 2% profit margin. If an inner-city store can charge 5% higher while keeping the same costs of business, then profit will have increased 250% [5% / 2% = 250%]. This high rate of profit will induce many others to open up shop, which will cause the price of goods to fall and the rate of profit to normalize. The tougher neighborhoods have higher prices and fewer stores because the crime makes the costs of business substantially higher.

Racial Segregation and the Free Market
The businessperson who seeks a profit is often dependent on minority customers. Businesses in a racially diverse area would not survive for long if they denied potential minority customers access to their premises, or humiliated them by making them drink at a separate water fountain or sitting in the back of the bus. It was, in fact, the government which created the so-called "Jim Crow Laws", segregating black and white people. These laws required legal segregation in public facilities, such as schools, bathrooms and transportation vehicles, with the justification that the facilities were "separate but equal."

It is important to note that the vast majority of blacks have never lived under a true capitalist system in the United States. They were heavily concentrated in the South as slaves, and once they were freed and started to move to other places around the country, the relatively free market was becoming more and more controlled by the government, particularly since the 1930's.

The European immigrants that came to America during the 1800's were greeted by a much freer society than that which greeted the masses of black people who moved from the South after WWII. Black people have been deprived of many of the benefits they would have enjoyed under the free market system, and have been made to suffer many of the ill effects of government legislation. While the intended purpose of the government may not be to suppress black people, unfortunately that is its effect.

Race and Unions

The purpose of unions is to raise the members' wages above market level. They are able to accomplish this goal through legislation and by forcing the employer to bargain and make concessions. This acts to reduce the amount of employees in the unionized industries because the employers have only so much money to spend. The higher wage rates also result in higher product prices, and a decreased supply of the good. The effect of businesses being legally compelled to deal with labor unions is to reduce the quantity of labor demanded, resulting in an artificial scarcity of jobs. There are more people willing to do the job than there are openings. The result is that some people are excluded, and because of the existing prejudice against black people, they are often the ones who get shut out.

Those who are not so fortunate as to have union jobs must find lower paying work. If they paid higher wages, the black people would have gone to those jobs first. These already lower wages get pushed even lower as they have to deal with the artificial increase in the supply of labor because of all of the people who are excluded from the unionized jobs.

This artificial wage reduction is a major factor in why the average black family income is substantially less than the average white family. In a completely free market, this could not exist. Under a true capitalist system, employers in the unionized industries would hire non-union black workers until their wage rates were equal to those of the unionized whites. However, under the current government, the National Labor Relations Board would levy large financial penalties against any employer who tried it. And with the 1973 Supreme Court *Enmons* decision exemption in their back pockets, the labor unions involved would be free to resort to violence and intimidation against the employer and the black people the employer tried to bring in.

This can greatly effect the psychology of a person, as the existence of such a system often acts to discourage black individuals from acquiring advanced skills for those jobs in the first place. Unfortunately, to the superficial observer it can appear that black people are in lower paying jobs simply because they do not have the skills for anything better.

Race and Minimum-Wage Laws
While unions force people into lower paying jobs, minimum-wage laws effect all types of labor, so there is nowhere else to go for those who are now excluded from working altogether, but to be on welfare. The impact of minimum-wage laws is greatest on the poorest, least educated and least skilled of the population. Since black people comprise a disproportionately large percentage of this population, they bare the worst brunt of the minimum-wage laws, which results in a much higher unemployment rate for black people than for white. The effect of this type of legislation is to reduce the income of many black people all the way down to zero, because they are legally barred from working since they are not allowed to compete on price.

Pro-union and minimum-wage laws work together to the detriment of many, but disproportionately the black people. Here are the chain of events: pro-union laws act to increase the supply of cheaper labor, and minimum-wage laws act to decrease that supply, resulting in large, unnecessary unemployment. They also have a long-term harmful effect: those who are excluded from the workforce altogether (many black teenagers) are not able to develop the skills and gain the knowledge for further advancement in the future. This effectively keeps them in the state of either being unemployed or fit for only the lowest-income labor.

Since these laws cause unemployment, there are welfare programs to help out those who cannot participate in the workforce. These

195

programs reduce people's incentive to work when their paycheck would be similar to or less than the welfare check. This system deprives these individuals of gaining skills on the job and moving up the economic ladder. You can see how the wage laws combined with the welfare programs tend to hold people back.

Race, Drugs and Crime

Wage laws and legislation which prevent adolescents from working combine to push poor, disproportionately black people, to look for other forms of income, even if they are illegal. The higher crimes rates of black people are not due to skin color, but are a combined result of having so many avenues for personal advancement cut off and the classification of producing, selling and using drugs as a crime.

In 2002, over 16% of local jail inmates said they committed their current offense to obtain money for drugs. In 2004, it was 17% of state prisoners and 18% of federal inmates. (James et al., 2005; Karberg et al., 2006) In 2006, black people were 6 times more likely to be the victim of homicide than white people, and 7 times more likely to be the one committing the homicide, per 100,000 population. A significant amount of homicides are drug-related.

What would happen if drugs were in the same legal category as alcohol, where abuse of them could become a medical and psychological problem, but not a criminal one? Fortunately we can learn from our experience with the prohibition of alcohol during the 1930's. At that time, it was not black people who were involved in the violence, it was largely the Italian mafia. Now that alcohol is legal, are people shooting one another over it anymore? While violence over alcohol during prohibition was common, nowadays it is virtually nonexistent. In the same way that the prohibition of alcohol led to higher rates of murder and incarceration related to the underground market of alcohol, the current prohibition of drugs has led to the same consequences.

Let me be clear that in making the case for drugs being legal, I am not encouraging their use. Those who do choose to partake would hopefully do so responsibly, but if they came to abuse it, they can be treated medically and psychologically, like alcoholics, rather than as criminals. If drugs were legalized, that would not give people free reign to do whatever they liked while using. Alcohol is legal for most people, but it is illegal to drive under the influence because it seriously endangers other people. Hammers are legal to own and use, but swinging them around wildly while walking down a crowded sidewalk would not be tolerated because it would be endangering people. The same would be true for drugs. Just as businesses often make their own rules about whether or not alcohol, cigarettes or even shoes are allowed on their premises, the use of drugs would have to be in alignment with the rules of the property owner, whether it is your own house, a park, a business or a sidewalk.

> Many politicians of our time are in the habit of laying it down as a self-evident proposition, that people ought not to be free till they are fit to use their freedom. The maxim is worthy of the fool in the old story, who resolved not to go into the water till he had learned to swim. If men are to wait for liberty till they become wise and good in slavery, they may indeed wait forever.
>
> Lord Macauley,
> British politician, 1847

While the cost of producing most illegal drugs is very low, their illegality combined with their high desirability to people allow the sellers to charge a price which is often hundreds of times the cost of production. If it costs about $2000 per week to support a strong drug habit, no poor person would be able to afford that from legitimate employment. This is why poor people often turn to burglary, violence and selling drugs in order to afford them.

However, if the drugs were legalized, they might cost about $20 per week, or even less. A poor person would not have to resort to selling drugs, burglary or violence in order to support that habit. So rather than someone being in possession of something which would land them in jail, and committing acts which would land them in jail, the person could be treated as a law abiding person with a possible medical or psychological problem. In order to support a $2000 per week drug habit, the criminal acts committed would have to be bigger and more often than those needed to support a $20 per week habit. It follows that legalizing drugs would dramatically reduce the amount of violence related to getting money for drugs.

The message that is promoted in the media is that it is one's environment that shapes what one can do. When people give up on the possibility of achieving anything through their own efforts, the higher crime rate in ghettos loses its mystery as drugs and crime seem to offer an escape. Hopefully you can see now that it is the government, not capitalism, that is the reason so many black people live in poverty.

MYTH: ONE PERSON'S GAIN IS ANOTHER'S LOSS

There is a common sentiment that rich people's wealth comes at the expense of everyone else's; that they are only able to live lavishly because others are forced to live in poverty. Many believe that in the free market, the fittest are able to climb to the top only by pushing the others down, in a law of the jungle system. Rather than allow businesses and property owners to profit off of other people, everyone should be an equal owner.

In a hunter-gatherer society, it would be survival of the fittest, and one person's gain would be another's loss because each person would be taking away resources when they consumed, but not adding to them. In the division of labor economy of a free market, one person is able to gain only by enriching the lives of others. As government intervention increases people are able to become wealthy by taking from others. In a truly free economy, rather than survival of the fittest people, it is the survival of the fittest products and services. So those goods which most satisfy people are able to continue their existence in the marketplace. Businesses become more successful by increasing productivity, which makes previous luxury items such as running water, electricity, cars, computers and cell phones available to the masses.

> Competition under capitalism is of an entirely different character than competition in the animal kingdom. It is not a competition for scarce, nature-given means of subsistence, but a competition in the positive creation of new and additional wealth, from which we all gain.
>
> George Reisman,
> American economist, 1981

But aren't the capital owners the primary beneficiaries of the capital they own? Consider who physically benefits from the ownership of Ford's auto manufacturing plants, International Paper's paper producing facilities, or Nike's shoe factories. It is the buyers of the products - automobiles, paper and shoes, respectively. The consumer gets the benefits of all of these factories simply by purchasing the end good. You don't have to own the company or even have any stock in it to benefit. When combined, the consumers get a much greater benefit than the capital owners themselves. In fact, the perceived value received by the consumers is greater than the total revenue of the business. Each time a consumer purchases something from a company, they believe they will value what they purchased more than the money given up. Therefore, collectively, the consumers received more value than they gave up in money, which is equal to the company's revenue.

The overwhelming majority of the benefit derived from the means of production are derived by non-owners in the form of wages, salaries and the goods and services that are sold. Not only do those in the public who do not own capital goods derive benefit from them, they also exert great control over them. The capital owner is not able to do as he or she pleases without concern for what the consumers want. The owner must be responsive to the wishes of the public or else the competition will get patronized, and his or her business will suffer.

There is a special benefit to owning capital goods - the previously produced factors of production - and that is the profit. When it is reported that a company made some huge sums of profit, many people may imagine the owners taking that money and buying yachts and planes and so forth. Most of the profit that a company makes though, is reinvested in order to maintain and grow the business. The actual percentage of the profit that the owners take for their own consumption is generally quite low. If they were to consume all of the profit, they would not be able to stay competitive, and since the replacement costs of capital goods tends to go up due to inflation, they would not have enough money to cover the rising costs of business. The special benefit is that small percentage of the profit that goes toward personal consumption.

Public ownership is supposed to give each of us a benefit we may not be able to get in the private ownership world. So each American is considered to be one 300-millionth owner of the United States Post Office, Amtrak, and government owned land which accounts for about one-third of the country. This sort of ownership confers no real benefit on each tax-payer for several reasons. Government-owned businesses are operated outside of the free market where profit and loss provide incentives for owners to improve their products and services to meet customer demands and stay competitive. Public ownership means that you have to pay for it whether you use it or not. You cannot take your money elsewhere, thereby sending the message that their business is not meeting the needs of the customers. Part of the definition of owning something is being able to disown it, but people are not able to sell their "share" of public property; they are forced to pay for it indefinitely. Rather than an owner, each tax-payer is more accurately called a forced subsidizer.

The extensive U.S. government land holdings in the Western states deprive individuals of making use of the natural resources The following are the percentages of government owned land in various states: Alaska: 89.22%; Arizona: 53.59%; California: 42.36%; Colorado: 39.86%; Idaho: 66.55%; Montana: 34.86%; New Mexico: 40.62%; Nevada: 81.07%; Oregon: 31.58%; Utah: 70.40%; Washington: 36.41%; Wyoming: 54.65%. When the government does hand out some permits for mining, grazing or logging, those are done in ways which are far less sustainable because each user does not care about the long term future given that they do not have long term contracts.

Any member of the "public" who thinks he owns the property may test his theory by trying to appropriate

for his own individual use his [portion] of
government property.

Murray Rothbard, American
philosopher and economist, 1962

Rather than taking their big chunk of change out of the pie, leaving
everyone else with less, ethical, successful capitalists increase the
supply of goods and services, effectively enlarging the size of the
pie by making each dollar more valuable. They are delivering
better products for lower prices, thereby raising your standard of
living.

MYTH: "FREE TRADE" AGREEMENTS ENSURE TRUE FREE TRADE

There is a fair amount of confusion about free trade because certain
government organizations have co-opted the term and used it for
regulated trade. Rather than allowing true economic freedom to
exist by eliminating government intervention, the North American
Free Trade Agreement (NAFTA), like the European Union, seeks to
control every matter, whether they are industrial, agricultural,
environmental or labor related. NAFTA is not, and never was,
about free trade - which is simply voluntary exchange of goods
and/or services between two or more parties, unhampered by
government intervention. The results of NAFTA are not increased
genuine free trade but the internationalization of the regulatory
structures, thus making the bureaucrats, which enforce the trade
laws under which people have to work, even less accountable to the
people of any given country.

NAFTA created many regulatory agencies and allowed for the
possibility of many more to be created. Before its enactment, trade
analyst Thomas Eddlem cautioned:

> Adoption of [NAFTA]... and its side agreements... will create a lot of new high-paying jobs. Unfortunately, most of them will be government positions for bureaucrats working in the more than 30 new international government committees, subcommittees, councils, working groups and subgroups mandated by NAFTA... NAFTA itself would establish the Free Trade Council - a continental government-in-waiting with enormous discretionary powers - with at least eight permanent committees, six 'working groups,' and five subcommittees and subgroups. NAFTA's side agreement on import surges would add a permanent 'Working Group on Emergency Actions,' and the side agreements on labor and the environment would create two additional regional law making bodies, each with its own bureaucracy and advisory committees. (Grigg, 2004)

In 2003, the Free Trade Area of the Americas was promoted on the basis that it would be the world's largest free trade region, encompassing 34 countries and approximately 800 million people. This sounds like a great win for everybody involved. Unfortunately, this and other "free trade" agreements are not intended to benefit the average person, but rather bolster the power of the political class.

The simplicity of true free trade eliminates the need for any government. If a free trade agreement were written up to express this, its length would probably be less than a page, and could even be summed up in just one sentence: *people's right to freely exchange their property with one another shall not be infringed upon.* So why then are these supposedly "free trade" agreements and structures many hundreds of pages long? Because the goal is not to have each person in control of their property, but rather to take that power one step further away from the individual, from the nation to the region, and ultimately under the direction of global government. Rather than being able to set your own rules, you must follow the dictates of a bureaucracy in charge of your entire hemisphere. Free trade simply cannot exist while a government exists, regulating what people can and cannot do. The opposite of that is true as well, that a government cannot exist if there is genuine free trade.

When regulation and taxation become too burdensome, many companies choose to move their production abroad to less legally suffocating places, resulting in a siphoning off of capital from the highly regulated and taxed places toward the less regulated and taxed places.

As you can see, the expression "free trade" has been co-opted. Many people are instinctively attracted to concepts like "free", "freedom" and "free trade" because each term implies that they are self-determined, and politicians realize that by using these words and phrases they can get people's support. The political class has twisted the meaning of this expression to mean countless supranational bureaucracies regulating and overseeing trade.

We must remember that, despite the "free trade" rhetoric, the purpose of the General Agreement on Tariffs and Trade (GATT), the World Trade Organization (WTO), the General Agreement on Trade and Services (GATS), the North American Free Trade Agreement (NAFTA), the Free Trade Area of the Americas (FTAA) and similar "free trade" agreements is not to promote prosperity, but rather to consolidate power. While true free trade would eliminate government and lead to a thriving economy, these international trade bureaucracies further separate people from their rights resulting in regional and then global socialism.

MYTH: EMPLOYERS CONTROL WAGE RATES

There is a common belief that if there were not "livable wage" regulations that employers would drive all wages down, until they were around subsistence level. It is thought that the employer holds the power in setting wages, and the combination of the boss's greed and the worker's need for a job would result in the pay spiraling downwards.

Superficially this makes some sense because people need to have some form of income to live, and if need be, people would be willing to work for minimum subsistence. On the other side, it is in the employer's best interest to pay the workers as little as possible. Putting these two pieces together, it seems that in the free market, employers would continue to push the wages down until they were at minimum subsistence.

However, someone's willingness to work for subsistence pay, and an employer's desire to pay as little as possible are *irrelevant* in the actual labor market. This is because far from there being a surplus of labor, it is actually the most useful and scarce thing in an economy. For all of the goods we could imagine purchasing, if only we had the money, labor is needed to create them. We can imagine far more uses for labor than can presently be satisfied. The other useful things in our economy, such as machines, factories, trucks, ships, etc., are all created by labor, and it is the limited supply of labor which limits the amount of these useful goods that are available. But wait, isn't it the supply of *money* which limits the supply of goods? If this were true, simply creating more money would allow for more products to be created. But as we have gone over this simply devalues the currency already in circulation.

This means that there is competition for workers. And it is this competition among employers over the limited supply of workers that raises the wages. As with any other good, the value of labor is determined by supply and demand. If someone has special skills, such as being a medical doctor or an outstanding athlete in a popular sport, they are part of a much smaller supply and are highly in demand, so their wages go up accordingly. Even though some employers would like to pay subsistence level wages to their workers, they must keep the wage high enough so that the employees will not just leave for a better opportunity.

Because labor is scarce, wage levels will not stay below the point reached when there is full employment in a free market. Why is this so? If the wages were at a certain level at full employment, and some businesses tried to lower the rate further, the result would be a labor shortage. At the lower wage rate the quantity of labor demanded would increase, but since the supply is the same, a shortage would ensue. If wages did fall below full employment levels, it would actually be in the best interest of the employers to raise the wage level until it was at full employment equilibrium. Until the wage rates did rise, there would be a shortage of employees. This shortage would naturally cause the wages to rise to the full employment level.

> The only means to raise wage rates permanently for all those eager to earn wages is to raise the productivity of labor by increasing the per-head quota of capital invested and improving the methods of production.
>
> Ludwig von Mises,
> *Planning for Freedom,* 1952

MYTH: AMERICAN CAPITALISM
WON THE BATTLE AGAINST COMMUNISM

Growing up around the time that Soviet Russia collapsed, I had little knowledge of foreign affairs, but a lot of people seemed very happy that the Berlin Wall was taken down. I kept hearing that communism was destroyed and that the American way of life had prevailed. While I didn't really know what that meant, I was glad to be on the winning side. As I learned more over the years, I found out that communism was an ideology based on centralized government control over the economy and people's lives, while the American tradition was claimed to be based upon life, liberty and the pursuit of happiness. When I came across those descriptions, I was even more thankful that the United States had not succumbed to communism.

In my mind, American policies and communist one's were nearly polar opposites, so it was to my great surprise when after reading the *Communist Manifesto*, by Karl Marx and Friedrich Engels, I noticed that several of the 10 Planks of Communism already had foundation in the United States. These were the 10 steps that Karl Marx described as necessary to destroy the free enterprise system. Upon further research, I found that to some degree all 10 of the Planks were already instituted in the U.S, some much more so than others. Unfortunately those which are most important to the success of communism are the ones which have been more fully incorporated into the American system.

If communism was dead, then what was going on here? This was an important piece of information for me to come upon because I had thought, as many others still do, that communism was an antiquated ideology that had failed. However, while the name "communism" may have died, the basic tenets of it are still alive.

Communism is not Russia, China, Cuba, Stalin, Zedong or Castro, it is an ideology which can just as easily go under different names. It is very easy to see if a person has beliefs which are in alignment with the *Communist Manifesto*: just think about whether the person wants the State or the free market to control the monetary system, commerce, communications, education and people's property. When you do this, all of a sudden people's "name tags" - their various political associations - fall away to reveal their underlying philosophy, whether that is capitalism or State-control. As I have shown throughout this book, private property rights are the backbone of prosperity, and it is the communist belief system which sets out to destroy that.

If we desire a better future then we must be clear about what is getting in the way of our progress.

FIRST PLANK: *Abolition of property in land and the application of all rents of land to public purposes.*
AMERICAN POLICY: Zoning laws and building permits force private property owners to get permission from the government regarding the use of their property. More than one-third of the country's land is now owned by the government: 26% federal, and close to 9% state. While private parties are able to lease some of the land for things such as mining, grazing and timber, the proceeds go to the U.S. Treasury. No one really owns their property because if you fail to pay your taxes (including your property tax), then the government will take your property (land, house, etc.). In 2005, the Supreme Court held in the Kelo v. City of New London case that the eminent domain clause could be used to transfer land from private owners to corporations against the owner's wishes.

SECOND PLANK: *A heavy progressive or graduated income tax.*
AMERICAN POLICY: The Corporate Tax Act of 1909. The 16th Amendment to the U.S. Constitution, allegedly ratified a tax on

incomes in 1913. The Revenue Act of 1913, section 2, Income Tax. The Social Security Act of 1935 - the payroll taxes for which are collected under the authority of the Federal Insurance Contributions Act.

THIRD PLANK: *Abolition of all rights of inheritance.*
AMERICAN POLICY: The Revenue Act of 1916 instituted the estate tax and 16 years later, the Revenue Act of 1932 introduced the gift tax to prevent people from trying to avoid the estate tax. The federal government imposes these transfers on wealth through its unified transfer tax system which is comprised of the estate tax, the gift tax, and the generation-skipping tax. There are also many state inheritance taxes as well.

FIFTH PLANK: *Centralization of credit in the hands of the State, by means of a national bank with State capital and an exclusive monopoly.*
AMERICAN POLICY: The Federal Reserve Banking System was established by the Federal Reserve Act in 1913. This is the central bank for the United States which controls the interest rate, and thereby the general supply of money.

SIXTH PLANK: *Centralization of the means of communications and transportation in the hands of the State.*
AMERICAN POLICY: This is a long list, so prepare yourself. The Radio Act of 1927 authorized the Federal Radio Commission to regulate radio use in the United States, which it did until it was replaced by the Federal Communications Commission in 1934; the Air Commerce Act of 1926 was the start of the regulation of aviation; the Civil Aeronautics Act of 1938 created the Civil Aeronautics authority to centralize regulation of civil air travel; the Federal Aviation Agency was created in 1958, later called the Federal Aviation Administration, which was empowered to take control of all of the navigable airspace over the United States for

both civilian and military purposes; in 1966, the FAA folded into the newly created Department of Transportation; the Federal-Aid Highway Act of 1916 made tax funds available to states for the construction of highways; and the Federal-Aid Highway Act of 1944 created the Interstate Highway System. We are fortunate that the internet is still unregulated, and we need to be vigilant about keeping it that way.

TENTH PLANK: *Free education for all children in public schools. Abolition of children's factory labor in its present form. Combination of education with industrial production.*
AMERICAN POLICY: In October of 1979, the Department of Education was created. Our public education is paid for through taxes; the Fair Labor Standards Act of 1938 set the "legal" minimum working age for most types of employment at 14, prohibited employing those under 18 in "dangerous" jobs, and limited the daily and weekly work hours of employees under 16.

Hopefully it is now clear that the communist ideology is neither strictly a foreign issue nor a deceased way of thinking. This ideology, which denies property rights and gives some people authority over others, goes by many different names. It is not important to remember the names though. What is important is that you be able to identify, when you watch the news or read an article, whether the person's worldview fundamentally is in alignment with property rights or not.

Chapter 8

WHERE DO WE GO FROM HERE?

As I have shown throughout this book, personal and economic freedom are critical in allowing people to spontaneously create a world in which we prefer to live. It is the harmony of people's self-interests which produces the food, houses, cars, books and music which enrich our lives. The fundamental distinction comes down to whether our needs and desires are met by violating other people's property rights or our rights are respected and our needs and desires are met peacefully. Advocating for a society based on aggression or based on liberty are our two options.

Fortunately, many people who have been on the side of advocating government control over much of our lives have been doing so without understanding the implications. It is my great hope that by making this distinction as clear as possible, each person can see that voluntary exchange is not only the nonviolent way but also the more effective way of achieving our common goals for the quality of our lives and for the health of environment.

The game between these two sides has been going on for ages, but more people are becoming aware of how controlled their lives are by other people. As increasing numbers of people wake up to this, the movement for complete personal and economic freedom gains power. This chapter looks at some possible next steps we can take.
In the same way that the economy cannot be run effectively by one person or a small group of people, the same is true of the

movement for personal and economic freedom. While I can lay out some pieces which I think are important steps, the movement will be far more effective if rather than looking up to someone else for all of the answers, we each take spontaneous, creative action because we are inspired to do so. Each person will bring something unique to the table, and there are so many ways that people can make a tremendous difference. So if you are inspired by the message in this book, get those creative juices flowing in your brain, start talking with friends, colleagues and family and take some sort of action, whether it is outlined in this book, you hear it from someone else, or you come up with an idea yourself.

> If there is no struggle, there is no progress. Those who profess to favor freedom and yet deprecate agitation are men who want crops without plowing up the ground.
>
> Frederick Douglass,
> Abolition leader, 1857

A BRIGHT POSSIBILITY

Early on in this book I had you envision a dark possibility, because I am afraid we are headed in that direction. I hope that through the rest of the book you have seen that neither oppression and destitution nor freedom and prosperity are inevitable. It is all up to us - to the beliefs that we have and the actions we take. The purpose of this book is to raise awareness so we can avert that dark future. With this raised awareness we have a different future to look forward to, and that is what I would now like you to envision.

A lot of this may be hard to imagine because we have become so used to living in a world of where the violence of government is used to solve social problems - it has become to us like water is to fish. Though I am contrasting this vision with the "dark possibility", this is by no means a utopia. This is not happy-land where everyone always gets along, all needs are always met and there is no crime. The point is that things would be much better, and the guiding principle of society would be one of nonviolence. Certainly there would still be some crime and corruption, but they could be dealt with much more swiftly and ethically than if these situations occurred where a government is present. When it is found out that a company is corrupt, customers will simply patronize the competition. Customers will reward companies which have integrity by purchasing their products and services.

Even though I do not foresee this as a utopia, it would be a lot closer to having people's needs met than in our present state. Let's start with how much wealthier everyone would be. Most of people's productivity is presently sucked away through taxes, inflation and regulatory compliance. Imagine that you are able to keep *everything* that you earned. So instead of working half of the year to pay taxes, you own it all and can do with it what you please.

But this is not just one person with some extra cash. Nearly everyone on the planet is affected by the current monetary system. The effect of this would be a massive increase in both capital investments and consumer spending, which would very quickly launch an era of prosperity beyond anything previously experienced.

There would be no initiation of force which would be legitimized. There would be few violent conflicts, starvation would be rare, medical and technological advancements would be rapid, allowing people to live longer, healthier lives. People would have the freedom to live their lives as they pleased so long as they did not initiate force against others.

Because people would no longer be subsidized not to work (welfare) or punished for working harder (progressive income taxes), they would have increased incentive to become more productive. When people become more productive, each dollar goes further. So instead of your income always trying to catch up to the rising cost of goods, your income would go further, purchasing more goods because the prices would be falling.

This is certainly a future which excites me.

BRINGING THE FUTURE INTO THE PRESENT

When I first wrote this chapter I thought about what the bright future could look like, and then I thought about all of the obstacles in the way, and the solutions I was championing were the removal of those obstacles. For example, getting rid of the Federal Reserve and government sanctioned fractional-reserve banking, abolishing protectionist laws, and abolishing taxes, etc. After the initial excitement of identifying those actions which needed to be taken before we could see a really free world, I had an overwhelming feeling of powerlessness. I realized that focusing on solving the big out-there problems was going to slow down this movement to a crawl. By attempting to have our actions first be on such a grand scale, we are skipping some important steps, namely looking at ourselves and our environment and identifying what made us support the system of coercion in the first place.

The approach which I feel better about now is to have that visualized future which excites each of us in our minds, and then step by step bring that future into the present. What are the actions each of us can take today which will result in the future we want to live in? By looking at the answers to this question, we are able to turn the seemingly insurmountable task of transforming the world into small, personal actions that we can take and make progress with in the short term.

To the early abolitionists and advocates of a heliocentric solar system, we are the future. We now live in a world where the type of slavery that was prevalent for ages is no longer tolerated, and it is the rare person who still believes that the Earth is the center of this solar system. We take this knowledge for granted now, but certainly appreciate the strides forward taken by those early agitators for truth and consistency.

Imagine having a conversation with your descendent at some point in the future when the world is finally rid of the myth of government authority, and she asks you how you were a part of the movement to free people. Will you answer that you kept quiet and conformed to social expectations or will you answer that you were courageous enough to have what were often times uncomfortable conversations with people, which helped to get the ball rolling?

I understand from personal experience how stressful it can be to bring these sorts of conversations up with people. If everyone were stopped by those fears then we wouldn't get any closer to complete liberty. We can't just wait for others to get the momentum going and then jump on when it's safe. We need to create that momentum ourselves and be that change we desire to see in the world.

WHAT CAN WE DO?

We need to establish having a truly free market as a conscious objective. It is our beliefs which ultimately shape the world in which we live, and it is our belief in and our obedience to people in government which gives it its power. We must mentally delegitimize government so that we see the bureaucrats like actors in a play and not as super humans, as many presently do.

If we do not think critically and we accept the socialist dogma, or if we continue to think that our best hope for our future is the "lesser of two evils", then most of us will end up suffering both the immediate and long term consequences. It is of utmost importance to envision the possibilities of this free market world and start taking action. The only thing standing in the way of our world being one of peace and voluntary exchange is that not enough people have understood the principles of liberty and been willing to take a stand.

We need to be committed to making this transformation to freedom as quickly as possible, even though this will likely be a long process. Imagine if slavery was still present in America the way it used to be. In our agitation for freedom for all, should we put together a 30-year or even a 10-year plan to gradually reduce our dependence upon slavery? Any long-term, gradual plan for abolishing slavery seems ludicrous because we would want it done as quickly as possible. Otherwise, we would be justifying the enslavement. When trying to extricate ourselves from our current slavery of government force, the same is true, that we want it done as readily as possible.

An important aspect in shifting from a government-centered society to a completely free market is personal responsibility. Rather than look toward the government for answers, solutions and saving, in the free market we become more self-reliant and more rational thinkers, while at the same time we become more interconnected with others.

The greatest challenge in reclaiming our rights is getting past the denial of what is really going on and taking responsibility for our own thoughts and actions. It takes tremendous courage to keep an open mind in the face of information which sharply conflicts with the worldview you have held. In order to create the world of peace and prosperity that many of us desire, it is in our best interest to see the truth even if it is contrary to what we have believed. While the thought of transforming the world to the vision we hold in our heads can be quite overwhelming, we must remember that this is not a burden resting on the back of an individual but rather an opportunity in which we can all participate.

CIRCLE OF INFLUENCE

I think it is important to focus on our circle of influence, which is where we will have the best chances of creating a lasting impact. It was from Stefan Molyneux that I first heard of a multi-generational solution to our hierarchical coercion-based society. It was depressing for me to hear such a profound thinker talk about long term solutions to problems I wanted overturned the next day. It would be nice if all we had to do to achieve freedom was check a box, but if it were that easy it would have been done already.

Since there is no quick-fix, I believe it comes down to education, and I don't mean in public schools. I'm talking about having conversations with our friends and family about what government is, what ethics are and where they come from, and what are nonviolent ways to resolve social problems. It is these sorts of conversations which will get many people to start thinking critically again, and to stop blindly accepting the dictates of authority.

Through the course of having many of these kinds of conversations, I've seen which approaches work for keeping the dialogue going and which do not. Here are a few suggestions as you go forth, excited about your newfound knowledge. Rather than telling someone the way things really are, be curious and ask questions. Get to know why they think the way they do. Invite the person into the conversation and be a partner with them on a journey for truth rather than being combative and adversarial. When talking about government actions, focus more on the underlying ethics rather than the policies themselves. And while one can easily be seduced into talking about national or global issues, my preference is to extrapolate up to there from the starting point of what works in our personal lives. Hopefully these tips can aid you in bringing up these often uncomfortable topics with those you care about in a peaceful and non-threatening way.

If someone in your life continually sides with status quo of aggression, despite your many reasoned attempts at sharing the nonviolent approach, then you may want to look at what you are getting out of that relationship. If we can't take principled stands with the people we know, the likelihood of having any impact on the big power structures is negligible. We cannot successfully take on government until we take on abusive relationships in our own life. I like to think of it as giving more time and energy to relationships which are grounded in ethics and withdrawing from ones where the other person is consistently advocating unethical actions.

Some things we can do for the advancement of freedom are actually the cessation of things we are presently doing. Government and much of the media have instilled in many people the knee-jerk reaction of proposing a government solution whenever a problem exists. If we can extricate ourselves from the idea that government solves problems, we will no longer go knocking on bureaucrats' doors begging them to take money from others to attempt a fix whenever problems arise.

Since the solution is long term and the medium is education and conversation, a key element is how children are reared. If children are raised to have blind obedience to their parents, they are much less likely to be critical thinkers when it comes to other forms of authority, such as government. However, if children are allowed to grow up with their curiosity and rationality being respected, then the population of people who can think for themselves will continue to grow. And if children are not taught to respect and obey arbitrary authority, government will be seen as legitimate by fewer and fewer people.

> From the first catch-phrases flung at a child to the last, it is like a series of shocks to freeze his motor, to undercut the power of his consciousness. "Don't ask so many questions, children should be seen and not heard!"—"Who are you to think? It's so, because I say so!"—"Don't argue, obey!"—"Don't try to understand, believe!"-—"Don't rebel, adjust!"—"Don't stand out, belong!"—"Don't struggle, compromise!" —"Your heart is more important than your mind!"—"Who are you to know? Your parents know best!"—"Who are you to know? Society knows best!"—"Who are you to know? The bureaucrats know best!"— "Who are you to object? All values are relative!"—"Who are you to want to escape a thug's bullet? That's only a personal prejudice!"
>
> Ayn Rand, *Atlas Shrugged*, 1957

While we will not see dramatic global change in the near future by focusing on our circle of influence, we will notice a positive shift in our own lives. At least I have, and I believe you will too. By bringing these conversations to people in my life, I have made new friends and gone to new depths with members of my family.

Ultimately, this is all about having control over yourself, your property and your life. It is remarkable what people can do when their rights are respected. This journey of civilization will only become more interesting, creative, prosperous and joyful so long as we remember to be vigilant in protecting what is rightfully ours.

It is my profound hope that after reading this book you will be able to think more critically about the headlines in newspapers and on television, have deeper discussions with your family and friends, and join the movement which empowers the individual and leads to true peace and prosperity. Throughout this book I have shown that the initiation of force is not necessary in order for people to improve their lives, and that nonviolence is actually the way by which we can best satisfy our needs and desires, ethically and sustainably.

IN APPRECIATION OF THE HUMAN SPIRIT

While being aware of the tragedies around the world and feeling compassion for those in difficult situations, I am also overwhelmed with a sense of awe at the creativity and productivity of humans. I take in the sights and sounds around me - the music I am listening to, the apartment building I am living in, my computer, the cars outside, the clothes that people walking by are wearing and the food they are eating - and I think about all of the people that worked together to manifest these goods. It really boggles and delights my mind. I am so appreciative of the human spirit, and our eternal quest to enrich our lives.

Everyone has inside of him a piece of good news. The good news is that you don't know how great you can be! How much you can love! What you can accomplish! And what your potential is!

Anne Frank,
Holocaust victim, 1929-1945

The Secrets to Nonviolent Prosperity

ENDNOTES

Anderson, Terry, and Dean Lueck. "Land Tenure and Agricultural Productivity on Indian Reservations." Journal of Law and Economics, 35 (1992): 427-54.

Anderson, Terry. "Conservation Native American Style." PERC Policy Series, PS-6. 1996. The Property and Environmental Resource Center. <www.perc.org/perc.php? subsection=6&id=651>.

Anderson, Terry, John Baden, Walter Block, Thomas Borcherding, John Chant, Edwin Dolan, Donald McFetridge, Murray Rothbard, Douglas Smith, Jane Shaw, and Richard Stroup. Economics and the Environment: A Reconciliation. Ed. Walter Block. Vancouver, BC: The Fraser Institute, 1990; pg. 293.

Anderson, Terry. "Self-Determination: The Other Path For Native Americans." PERC Reports: The Magazine of Free Market Environmentalism June 2006: 4.

Armentano, Dominick T. Antitrust : The Case for Repeal. Annapolis: Ludwig von Mises Institute, 1999.

Associated Press. "Shot Hits Another Greyhound Bus As a 'Possibility' of Talks Arises." 13 Mar. 1990. The New York Times. <http://query.nytimes.com/gst/fullpage.html? res=9c0ce6d91238f930a25750c0a966958260>.

Bartlett, Bruce. "How Excessive Government Killed Ancient Rome." The Cato Journal, 14 (1994).

Bastiat, Frederic. The Law. Upper Saddle River: Foundation for Economic Education, Incorporated, 1996.

Benson, Bruce. "Property Rights and the Buffalo Economy of the Great Plains." In Self-Determination: The Other Path For

Native Americans. Ed. Terry Anderson, Thomas Flanagan
and Bruce Benson. Stanford, CA: Stanford UP, 2006.

Boaz, David. Libertarianism. New York: Simon & Schuster,
Incorporated, 1997; pg. 141.

Bonta, Steve. Inside the United Nations. New York: John Birch
Society, 2003.

Brown, Ellen Hodgson. Web of Debt (Revised and Updated) : The
Shocking Truth about Our Money System and How We Can
Break Free. New York: Third Millennium P, 2008.

Burris, W. Alan. A Liberty Primer. Washington D.C.: Society for
Individual Liberty of the Genesee Valley, 1983.

Callahan, Gene. Economics for Real People : An Introduction to
the Austrian School. Annapolis: Ludwig von Mises
Institute, 2004.

DiLorenzo, Thomas J. "Why Socialism Causes Pollution." The
Freeman 42 (1992).

"Drug use and Crime." Bureau of Statistics. U.S. Department of
Justice. <http://www.ojp.usdoj.gov/bjs/dcf/duc.htm>, 14
Aug. 2008.

Editorial. "Protected Thuggery." The Wall Street Journal 9 Sept.
1997.

Flyvbjerg, Bent, Mette Holm, and Soren Buhl. "Underestimating
Costs in Public Works Projects: Error or Lie?" Journal of
American Planning Association 68 (2002): 279-95.

Gatto, John. The Underground History of American Education. The
Oxford Village P, 2001.

Goklany, Indur. The Improving State of the World : Why We're
Living Longer, Healthier, More Comfortable Lives on a
Cleaner Planet. Annapolis: Cato Institute, 2006.

Gordon, David. An Introduction to Economic Reasoning.
Annapolis: Ludwig von Mises Institute, 2000.

Griffin, G. Edward. The Creature from Jekyll Island : A Second
Look at the Federal Reserve. New York: American Media,
1998.

Grigg, William Norman. America's Engineered Decline. New York: John Birch Society, 2004; Pgs. 40-41.

Hazlitt, Henry, and Steve Forbes. Economics in One Lesson. Little Rock: Fox & Wilkes, 1996; pg. 36.

Higgs, Robert. Against Leviathan : Government Power and a Free Society. Annapolis: The Independent Institute, 2004.

"Homicide Trends in the U.S.: Trends by Race." Bureau of Statistics. U.S. Department of Justice. <http:// www.ojp.usdoj.gov/bjs/homicide/race.htm#vrace>, 11 July 2007.

Hoppe, Hans-Hermann. Democracy - The God That Failed : The Economics and Politics of Monarchy, Democracy and Natural Order. New York: Transaction, 2001.

Hoppe, Hans-Hermann. The Economics and Ethics of Private Property. Annapolis: Ludwig von Mises Institute, 2006.

Ikenson, Dan. Ending the "Chicken War": The Case for Abolishing the 25 Percent Truck Tariff. Issue briefNo. 17. Center for Trade Policy Studies, Cato Institute. Washington D.C.: Cato Institute, 2003.

Institute for Justice. "Kelo v. New London: Lawsuit Challenging Eminent Domain Abuse in New London, Connecticut." 2009. <http://www.ij.org/index.php? option=com_content&task=view&id=920&Itemid=165>

James, Doris J.; Karberg, Jennifer C. "Substance Dependence, Abuse, and Treatment of Jail Inmates, 2002". Bureau of Justice Statistics. <http://bjs.ojp.usdoj.gov/index.cfm? ty=pbdetail&iid=1128>, July 2005.

Jasper, William F. The United Nations Exposed. Ed. Gary Benoit and Tom G. Gow. New York: John Birch Society, 2001; pgs. 121-123; 233.

Johnson, Bruce. "A Modern Potlatch?: Privatizing British Columbia Salmon Fishing." PERC Reports: The Magazine of Free Market Environmentalism, June 2006: 15.

Karberg, Jennifer C.; Mumola, Christopher J. "Drug Use and Dependence, State and Federal Prisoners, 2004." Bureau of Justice Statistics. <http://bjs.ojp.usdoj.gov/index.cfm?ty=pbdetail&iid=778>, Oct. 2006.

Kendrick, David. Freedom from Union Violence. Rep.No. 316. National Institute for Labor Relations Research. Washington D.C.: Cato Institute, 1998.

Kendrick, David. Violence: Organized Labor's Unique Privelege. National Institute for Labor Relations Research. Springfield, VA, 1996.

Kennedy, David M. "Who Owns the West?" Stanford Magazine. Stanford University. <http://www.stanfordalumni.org/news/magazine/2008/mayjun/features/west.html>, May-June 2008.

Kershaw, Peter. Economic Solutions. Englewood, CO: Quality P, 1997.

Kochan, Donald. Reforming Property Forfeiture Laws to Protect Citizens' Rights: Why and How to Curtail Abuses of Laws that Permit Private Property Seizures. Rep.No. Midland, MI: Mackinac Center for Public Policy, 1998.

Laband, David. "Water Shortage?" Ludwig von Mises Institute. <http://mises.org/story/526>, 13 Oct. 2000.

Lomborg, Bjorn. The Skeptical Environmentalist : Measuring the Real State of the World. New York: Cambridge UP, 2001.

Lucas, Fred. "Value of 2008 Bailouts Exceeds Combined Costs of All Major U.S. Wars." <http://www.freerepublic.com/focus/f-news/2160905/posts>, 18 Dec. 2008.

Marx, Karl, and Friedrich Engels. The Communist Manifesto. Grand Rapids: Filiquarian, LLC, 2007.

Mises, Ludwig von. Human Action: a Treatise on Economics. New Haven: Yale UP, 1949.

Mises, Ludwig von. The Theory of Money and Credit. Von, Mises Ludwig. New Haven: Yale UP, 1953.

Mises, Ludwig von, Gottfried Haberler, and Murray Newton

Rothbard. The Austrian Theory of the Trade Cycle and Other Essays. Annapolis: Ludwig von Mises Institute, 1996.

Mises, Ludwig von. The Quotable Mises. Ed. Mark Thornton. Annapolis: Ludwig von Mises Institute, 2005.

Molyneux, Stefan. Everyday Anarchy. <www.freedomainradio.com/books.html>, 2008.

Money as Debt. Dir. Paul Grignon. DVD. 2006.

The Money Masters. Dir. Bill Still. DVD. 2003.

Murphy, Robert P. The Politically Incorrect Guide to Capitalism. Boston: Regnery, Incorporated, An Eagle Company, 2007.

NotHaus, Bernard Von, ed. The Liberty Dollar : A Solution to the Federal Reserve. New York: American Financial P, 2003; pg. 61-63.

Orwell, George, Thomas Pynchon, and Erich Fromm. 1984. New York: Plume, 2003.

Perkins, John. Confessions of an Economic Hit Man. New York: Berrett-Koehler, Incorporated, 2004.

Prechter, Robert. "Gas Shortage: Irrational Herding or Economics?" Ludwig von Mises Institute. <http://www.mises.org/story/3136>, 8 Oct. 2008.

"Race, Prison and the Drug Laws." Drug War Facts. Common Sense for Drug Policy. <http://www.drugwarfacts.org/racepris.htm>, 2 Jan. 2008.

Rand, Ayn. Atlas Shrugged. Random House, 1957; pg. 996.

Reisman, George. Capitalism : A Complete and Integrated Understanding of the Nature and Value of Human Economic Life. New York: Jameson Books, Incorporated, 1997; pg. 589, 593.

Reisman, George. "Inflation and Price Controls, Disk 1." George Reisman's Program of Self-Education in the Economic Theory and Political Philosophy of Capitalism: Lectures and Speeches on Economics and Politics, 1967-2003. MP3. The Jefferson School of Philosophy, Economics and Psychology, Recorded 1976.

Rehmke, Gregory F. "Who is Destroying the Rainforests?" The Freeman: Ideas on Liberty. Reprinted online at <http:// w w w . e c o n o m i c t h i n k i n g . o r g / e n v i r o n m e n t / rehmkerainforest.html>, Nov. 1989.

Rockwell, Llewellyn H. The Economics of Liberty. Annapolis: Ludwig von Mises Institute, 1990.

Rothbard, Murray Newton. America's Great Depression. Annapolis: Ludwig von Mises Institute, 2000.

Rothbard, Murray Newton, and Joseph Stromberg. Man, Economy, and State with Power and Market : The Scholars Edition. Annapolis: Ludwig von Mises Institute, 2004.

Rothbard, Murray Newton. The Case Against the Fed. Annapolis: Ludwig von Mises Institute, 1994.

Rothbard, Murray Newton. What Has Government Done to Our Money? Annapolis: Ludwig von Mises Institute, 2005.

Rummel, R.J. "20th Century Democide." <http://www.hawaii.edu/ powerkills/20TH.HTM>, 2002.

Sammon, Bill. "Workers Report Union Violence." The Washington Times. <http://electric-america.com/wt98/wt0412t.htm>, 10 April, 1998.

Sandefur, Timothy. Cornerstone of Liberty : Property Rights in 21st Century America. Annapolis: Cato Institute, 2006.

Schiff, Irwin A., and Vic Lockman. How an Economy Grows and Why It Doesn't. New York: Freedom Books, 1985.

Schiff, Irwin A. The Social Security Swindle : How Anyone Can Drop Out. New York: Freedom Books, 1984.

Sennholz, Hans. "How to Create an Energy Crisis." The Free Market 19 (2001).

Shaw, Michael, Randy T. Simmons, and Carl P. Close. "Bureaucracy vs. the Environment: What Should be Done?" The Independent Institute. <http://www.independent.org/ events/transcript.asp?eventid=119>, 28 June, 2006.

Simon, Julian L. The Ultimate Resource 2. New York: Princeton UP, 1998.

Smith, Ray A. "Home Owners Revolt Against Tax Assessors." The Wall Street Journal Online. The Wall Street Journal. <http://www.realestatejournal.com/buysell/taxesandinsurance/20050202-smith.html>, 2 Feb. 2005.

Soto, Hernando de. The Mystery of Capital. New York: Basic Books, 2000.

Soto, Hernando de. The Other Path : The Invisible Revolution in the Third World. New York: Basic Books, 2002.

Stossel, John. "Foreign Aid Will Cure Poverty. Myth or Fact?" ABC News: John Stossel Video. <http://abcnews.go.com/2020/stosselvideo/>.

Vigilante, Richard. Strike : The Daily News War and the Future of American Labor. New York: Simon & Schuster, 1994.

Walker, Francis A. Money. New York, NY: H. Holt and Co., 1878. 337.

White, Andrew Dickinson. Fiat Money Inflation in France. 1896; pg. 8.

Williams, Walter. "Where Union Power Lies." Jewish World Review. <http://www.jewishworldreview.com/cols/williams101598.asp>, 15 Oct. 1998.

INDEX

FURTHER RESOURCE RECOMMENDATIONS

Bastiat, Frederic. The Law. Upper Saddle River: Foundation for Economic Education, Incorporated, 1996.

Callahan, Gene. Economics for Real People : An Introduction to the Austrian School. Annapolis: Ludwig von Mises Institute, 2004.

Gordon, David. An Introduction to Economic Reasoning. Annapolis: Ludwig von Mises Institute, 2000.

Hoppe, Hans-Hermann. The Economics and Ethics of Private Property. Annapolis: Ludwig von Mises Institute, 2006.

Lomborg, Bjorn. The Skeptical Environmentalist : Measuring the Real State of the World. New York: Cambridge UP, 2001.

Molyneux, Stefan. Books and Podcasts at www.Freedomainradio.com; Recommended: Everyday Anarchy, Practical Anarchy and Universally Preferable Behavior.

Rand, Ayn. Atlas Shrugged. Random House, 1957.

Reisman, George. Capitalism : A Complete and Integrated Understanding of the Nature and Value of Human Economic Life. New York: Jameson Books, Incorporated, 1997.

Rothbard, Murray Newton, and Hans-Hermann Hoppe. The Ethics of Liberty. New York: New York UP, 2003.

Rothbard, Murray Newton. What Has Government Done to Our Money? Annapolis: Ludwig von Mises Institute, 2005.

Made in the USA
Las Vegas, NV
25 October 2021

33073680R00138